high society ◉

the real voices of club culture

edited by melissa harrison

PIATKUS

NOTICE:

High Society is a collection of accounts submitted to Piatkus Books by members of the public and does not represent the views of the publisher or editor. It is a criminal offence to possess or supply any controlled substance and the publisher and editor do not condone or encourage any criminal activity described in this book.

First published in 1998 by
Judy Piatkus (Publishers) Ltd
5 Windmill Street
London W1P 1HF

The moral right of the editor has been asserted

A catalogue record for this book is available from the British Library

ISBN 0 7499 1783 0

Designed by the Senate

Data capture and manipulation by Phoenix Photosetting, Chatham, Kent
Printed and bound in Great Britain by Mackays of Chatham PLC,
Chatham, Kent

from the editor

High Society was conceived out of a growing sense of frustration with the way in which the mainstream media consistently misrepresent club culture and the dance music scene.

Despite the growing debate about the value of this cultural phenomenon, the numbers joining its ranks grows every year and its influence is now felt in the fields of art, fashion, literature and the media, not to mention music. There is no escaping it: for better or worse, the club scene is now a major part of British youth culture and deserves to have its own voice.

These stories demonstrate the true nature of the scene, and the different meanings it holds for those who are part of it. From a night out getting off your face to a way of recreating the social stability and sense of community a whole generation have grown up without; from pre-millennial escapism to hedonism, pure and simple, here are some very different voices telling very different stories.

Thanks to all the people who took the time to tell me their stories; they were great fun to read. Many people's efforts went above and beyond the call of duty; Jake, for starters, Colin, Simon, Ralf, Russell and most importantly, Jez. Thank you.

The devil has all the best tunes.
– proverb

Contributions for *High Society* were sent in in response to a competition we ran in several national music magazines to find the best clubbing story. The winner is Russell David for his account of his trip to New York to see Junior Vasquez play The Tunnel club. It appears on p.206.

contents

foreword

Billy Nasty is an internationally famous DJ and celebrity. He's seen dance music develop from the Rare Groove and Hip Hop sounds of 1986 to today's eclectic scene. He bought his first set of decks at 16, started DJing professionally in 1989 and was the first DJ to release a mix CD (JDJ vol. I). He can currently be found DJing all over Europe and the world as well as running his record label, Tortured Records, and overseeing Theremin Management which he set up to further the careers of young up-and-coming DJs. He was born and bred in London, where he still lives.

Reading through these experiences of others has triggered off memories of my own experiences that I had whilst still a teenager, mad for music and clubs and this whole new amazing secret world I'd discovered. I knew I had to get involved with it and try to help it grow by introducing my friends to it. Really I owe everything I have now to the DJs I used to dance and scream to when I was a young trainspotting clubber, desperate to become a part of the scene. They were my inspiration and I always hope that I can inspire others. I wasn't skilled in any other career before DJing, but I'd always had a very strong love of music. Because of the impact which clubs, music and DJing had on me from an early age, I knew this was what I definitely wanted to do, and this thirst and eagerness was the only thing I needed to get where I am today.

It is this philosophy that has attracted me to this book; the Acid House philosophy of getting up there and having a go yourself and striving to do what you feel is your best. One of the best things about the current dance music scene is the DIY culture which means anyone can get involved in any number of ways, from DJing and producing to the countless people behind the scenes – promotions companies, record shops, clubs, labels – and of course the most important people, the clubbers themselves.

The clubbers who have contributed to this book are, like myself, not professional journalists or authors, and because of this I've found their tales to be all the more honest and convincing. For anyone who has any experience of modern-day clubbing, these stories will ring a familiar bell. Every regular clubber has had their lives changed through the dance music scene in one way or another, and this collection of memories and experiences, good times and bad, will no doubt be referred to in years to come as an insight into the origins of the scene as we know it today. I will be including this book in my own personal time capsule, so in the future if my daughter, who is at the time of writing just four months old, asks me what I did when I was younger I'll unlock it and show her this book along with records, mix CDs of mine, press cuttings etc. and I hope that she will be able to see just how proud I was to be involved with it all.

Parents and politicians would do well to read this with an open mind. It might help them to understand a youth movement which isn't just about death, drugs and crime, the way it is often reported by the mainstream media. What is rarely reported, perhaps because it is such a difficult thing to describe, is the range of emotions it's possible to go through in the course of one evening's entertainment, and of course what a bloody laugh it all is. But also more importantly than that, this whole scene – now over a decade old – has helped bring together so many different kinds of people who would otherwise have had nothing in common. The creativity and constant growth of the scene amongst people worldwide who are now as passionate about clubs and music as I was aged sixteen, surely make this the first youth culture to go truly global.

do you

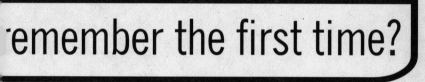

remember the first time?

Those were the days, man. Or more accurately, those were the nights. Nights of hardcore raving, '91-style, back when the world and we were young. Full on, radio-fucking-rental business. This is how it was . . .

It had taken us a long time to get around to all this dance music malarkey. We were all long-haired hippy/goth/skater types and although we'd all been students in Manchester through the time of the acid house thing, it had largely passed us by. But gradually our tastes had changed. As we got older and smoked more dope, we went from the mission and Slayer to Hawkwind, Culture Shock and dub, and from there to The Shamen, The Orb, Deee-Lite and the odd acid track: 'Humanoid' by Stakker, 'Acid Rock' by Rhythm Device, 'Yaah' by D-Shake, 'Voodoo Ray'. Remember those 'Acid: the music not the drug' T-shirts? It was kind of the other way round with us, at first. But the more of this dance stuff we heard, the more we understood it: loud, fast music full of weird noises that sounded good when you were tripping? Yeah, we could get to that.

So at the beginning of '91 a few friends started snorting a bit of speed and going to rave nights at the Academy; I thought they were being a bit daft, myself, and never bothered. Then it was summer. I graduated that year and spent summer on the dole, smoking lots of dope, taking lots of trips and generally having a bit of a beezer time, culminating in an intense mushroom season in October. And one thing we talked a lot about was how we'd like to go to a proper rave – none of us had ever really done it.

And we all fancied checking out what E was like. We'd smoked dope, taken mushrooms and LSD, snorted speed – ecstasy seemed like a logical progression.

It was time.

I wasn't one of the first in the group to go down to the PSV – don't know why, maybe I was going somewhere else, or I didn't have any money. Whatever, everyone came back full of enthusiasm the next day: *Absolutely brilliant. We're going again next week! You've gotta come.* So the next week I let myself be dragged along – not that I needed too much persuasion.

And fuck me! I'd never seen anything like it. Really. The music, the lights, the strobes, the MC ... but mostly, the people. Everyone was dancing – not like in the alternative clubs we were used to, get up and have a groove to a song or two you liked and sit down again, but going for it big time: dancing for five or six hours, tops off, sweating like fuck ... and everyone with these big pool-ball eyes, huge grins, complete strangers coming up to you, *Where ya from? What y'on? Y'having a good night?* No one wanted a battle. No one was pissed and falling all over you. All anyone wanted to do was dance.

Needless to say, we went back the week after. And the week after that. And the week after that ... The first few weeks I stuck to the speed, but it wasn't long before my best mate and I had our first pills. The Saturday-night pattern was well established by now. All gather round Pete's at eight o'clock; drink beer and smoke spliffs till they come out of your ears, till it was only about nine and you were so fucked you hardly thought you could go out at all – and then the drugs would arrive. A gram of speed, an E, maybe a quarter of a tab of acid. Phone for taxis round about nine thirty: I think the record was seven cabs, that's twenty-eight people. We'd stop off first at Stu's, who lived in a flat two minutes' walk from the club, to drop off clean T-shirts, jumpers, cans of beer for after . . .

By the time we got to the club, sometimes there'd be forty of us. Get a can of Red Stripe while you waited for the Es to kick in – you might get two down you sometimes, but once the pill started working it was on to the bottled water. And then you'd dance till you thought you were going to explode – the music was hardcore in varying shades, some weeks earbleeding Belgian stuff, other weeks more piano-y and even chart stuff, 'Insanity' and 'Such a Good Feeling' and 'Playing with Knives', but there was no snobbishness about it, no stupid subdivisions, it was just rave music. Our music. And still those pool-ball-eyed, grinning, friendly people.

Then when you needed a rest you'd wander up to the upstairs bar. The PSV was a well dodgy club, all kinds of dealers and gangsters in there, and going up the stairs you were running a bit of a gauntlet, but generally you didn't care – you were flying, no one could touch you, and anyway, why would anyone want to? The world was a beautiful place! You had to be careful in the bar, there were lots of Moss Side homeboys with short tempers around, but down at one end was where we always sat in a little alcove, and there was always someone there (out of the forty of you): someone to rabbit at if you had a mad speed head on, someone to give you a big reassuring hug if it was all getting a bit much, someone to give you a relaxing face rub if you started to sledge ... and you could skin up with impunity.

Whatever you were up to, the unspoken rule was that everyone went downstairs for the last half-hour, and that's when the club was really rocking ... they always used to end with 'So Real' by Love Decade, and I remember one time, I was kind of separated from my friends, I had my hands in the air (like everyone else) and someone grabbed one of them. I looked and it was some lad I'd never seen before, and then his mate grabbed my other hand, all of us with our shirts off, hug, and I swear, I wasn't the only one with tears in my eyes. This was it! This was what it was all about! We were in Manchester, the centre of the whole thing as far as we could see, and we were in the PSV, the most full-on club in Manchester. *The world is listening ... feel the power.* Indeed.

After the club it was back to Stu's to change into dry clothes, pick up the beers, and head off to a party. There was always a party somewhere, and we'd walk there, even if it was a couple of miles; you could safely walk through Moss Side when there was thirty of you, something you wouldn't do on your own at that time of night. And after the party, back to Pete's for yet more reefer, till some time in the late morning I'd leave there and stumble back to my own house round the corner and try to sleep. Not always with much success.

After a year or so the PSV started to go off a bit (too many shootings outside, too many people getting taxed inside, too many CS gas attacks) and we went off to fresh pastures: some people sticking with the underground techno parties in fields and squats and giving up clubs altogether, me personally discovering all-nighters at gay clubs where they played hardcore alongside what I was learning to call deep house and where the poppers kept you going till six a.m. The good times carried on – and they still do.

But there was something about those days: the bobble hats, the whistles, the Vicks (we actually favoured Olbas oil or Tiger Balm but they all did the same thing, they all heightened those rushes), the strangers sharing their water ... maybe it was just because it all felt so new, and we had so few worries. We didn't have all the examples of people necking pills and dropping dead; there weren't loads of people who'd given it all up because it was doing their head in – most of the original E-heads of '87 to '89 were still at it. We were young, we were happening, we were the whistle posse and we made some fucking noise whenever the MC wanted us to. We were it, man. The posse knew who the posse was and the posse looked out for each other. We were happy, carefree and off our heads. High society indeed.

Russell David, Bath

I'd like to tell you about the first time I went clubbing at Christmas.

Christmas clubbing is, I think you'll agree, a totally different experience. For a start, it's a completely different crowd. Most people are at home with their families and so the student population and the coupled-up population are to a large extent absent from the nation's dancefloors. This leaves the real heads, the real up-for-it don't-give-a-shit twenty-something couldn't-care-less crowd and that makes for a whole new atmosphere.

Secondly, like New Year there's an actual reason to party, apart from the fact that it's the weekend so everyone's really determined to live it up. It's the festive season; people are off work, in the Christmas spirit, and go out perhaps with a different attitude than they might during the rest of the year.

This particular year was also the first year I went out totally straight. I don't mean in terms of orientation, as I am as camp, as the saying goes, as Christmas itself, but I mean in terms of 'stimulants'. This was a few years ago, and I still don't do anything except smoke draw now and again. I've been there and done the whole lot and frankly I'd got bored of it. You hear everyone saying that the Es you get now aren't as good as in 'the good old days' and now that's become received wisdom but I'm here to tell you kids it's true. Words can't describe the feeling of the really pure Es we used to get when the scene first took off, back when 'house' meant 'queers' music' and before the money-makers stepped in. When the quality of pills nose-dived I used to supplement them with speed and coke, just like you do today children, but after a while I reached a point where I felt I had to make a choice and I made it.

I think most people who take clubbing seriously wake up one day and find they are on the point of 'living the scene': now we all know people who do this, don't we? They take shitty jobs just to pass the week or sign on so as to have enough money for their drugs for the weekend, which is all they're living for. It used to be called 'dropping out' and there is a point when your perspective shifts slightly and you realise your clubbing life, your clubbing self, is more important and more central to your perception of yourself as an individual than the rest of your day-to-day dreary life. Things like ambition, career goals, motivation, even family in bad cases can go out of the window. The diva on the dancefloor on a Saturday night is the real you and all the rest is just window dressing. This may be more prevalent in the gay scene, I don't know, as it's all caught up with other concepts such as being 'out on the scene' and your gay identity and such like.

In any case, it is very seductive and very dangerous and one day I found myself at that point and recognised it and had a long hard think to myself. And I decided that the weekday me was to be the real, primary me and the vision of loveliness you may be privileged enough to see one day on the dancefloor was strictly an alter ego and a weekend thing. And so I decided, as part of my resolution, to try going out without drugs, to see if that helped make the whole thing easier. As I said, I was getting a little bored anyway with the extortionate prices, frequent rip-offs, bad come-downs and the mid-week blues. The famous ecstasy deaths didn't affect my decision; most people I know see them as the result of naïve and irresponsible recreational drug use, not recreational drug use *per se*. People are more concerned that they might be being sold shit or that what their drugs are cut with might cause them to have a bad night out or cause spots or bad skin or give them kidney-ache and stop them dancing. And no one really worries about getting in trouble with the long arm of the law as we don't really see what we're doing as illegal. We're just going out and partying; drug abuse is things like heroin.

Anyway, the night I chose to put my resolution to the test was Christmas Eve. God knows why; I was risking a dreadful Christmas but there you have it!

I went out with my better half at the time and some old friends of ours to a gay club in Leeds. There isn't much of a gay scene in Tyne & Wear, as you might expect, and we're used to having to travel. We'd decided to stay in a hotel in Leeds for Christmas, the whole lot of us; we'd been spending the festive season together for a while. Family times are often difficult if you're gay as bringing your partner home isn't always an option and we'd decided long ago to cut out losses and party together every Christmas.

The club was decked out with fantastically tacky decorations and it was full of Santas and Christmas-tree fairies and Santa's little helpers – darlings, you can just imagine! The guys I was with had taken their pills in the queue and were coming up and I knew this was the worst bit – watching them come up and get loved up and not coming up myself. I knew if I started to feel excluded then it would persist all night so I flatly refused to give it a chance. I swiped their drinks off them, drank them all and then dragged my boys on to the heaving sweaty dancefloor as the DJ added some serious Latin beats into the mix. This caused them to come up immediately but we were all there together and I'd taken the initiative, and as we began to grin at each other and dance together I knew it would be all right.

I won't say any of those old clichés like you don't need drugs to have a good time, because sometimes you do. But I found out that night you don't *always* and that a brilliant night out is more to do with the right attitude than anything else. How often have you taken the same amount of drugs you usually do but still had a dreadful time? It happens to us all because however much you take it's your mood that determines if you have a fantastic evening or not. So, if you make sure your mood is right and you are in good physical shape you can go out 'straight' and last the night and have fun.

I don't go out every weekend now, not because I don't do the drugs when I go but because I'm happily 'married' and working on my house, or should I say our house! But I drag myself out at least once a month and party with the best, live it up a little and prove to myself that I'm not past it and that I've still got enough stamina to enjoy a wonderful night out without drugs.

Jean-Claude, Tyne & Wear

The first outdoor event I went to was Tribal Gathering and it was an amazing experience. At twenty-three, I am too young to have been part of the rave scene of 1988 and 1989, and although I go clubbing regularly I hadn't been to any big outdoor parties or festivals so it was all new to me. And although there are always people who tell you the dance music scene isn't anything now compared to what it used to be, and that events like Tribal Gathering are commercialised and a sell-out, I still had the best time of my life.

The train to Luton was full of people obviously on their way to Tribal. We sat amongst families and business travellers, clearly people with a common purpose, responding to their puzzled looks with enigmatic stares and to each other's glances of recognition with nods and smiles. I'd been looking forward to this weekend for so long I'd got to the point where I almost didn't want to go; I didn't think it could possibly live up to my expectations.

By the time my other half and I got off the train and on to the coach I was feeling irritable, I was so keyed up. It felt strange to be going out in the middle of the day; going out in the evening is a ritual I'm more used to: you pass the day in anticipation of the night ahead, you start getting ready as the evening programmes start on the TV and the radio starts playing dance music, and you go out in the dark, with a night of hedonism ahead of you. It was a hot day, and very bright, and here we were on a coach in the middle of beautiful countryside and I was finding it hard to get on the right vibe. Moreover, the closer we got to Luton Hoo the more security we were seeing by the side of the road, in the fields, with dogs ... I was carrying all our drugs and I was a wee bit concerned. I tried to push the thought to the back of my mind; there was no point worrying, I knew.

In the event we didn't even get searched (thank God). We went straight in and began to explore the massive site.

It took a while for me to get my bearings. It was a beautiful setting: a secluded valley, ringed with trees, with the imposing structure of the mansion visible from the drive into the estate. The tents were set in a rough circle, each one big enough to feel from the inside like a self-contained club in itself. The hardest tent, the one playing Detroit techno (where Jeff Mills – all hail the master – played) had corrugated iron around the entrances as well; this acted like a sound baffle as well as contributing to that minimalist techno feel.

There were also stands selling all kinds of food, clothes, jewellery, smart drinks, you name it; a phone cabin, the Samaritans (festival branch), medics, a chill-out tent, the Barefoot Doctor's Healing Oasis tent and God knows what else. It was whilst counting up the number of different cuisines available that we discovered that we had only a few quid between us to last until Sunday. This led to our desperate chewing of king-size Mars Bars later that afternoon (not a pleasant experience when large amounts of base speed have left you with only a vague memory of the concept of saliva). At least the water was free, although a little suspect as proximity to a running tap seemed to make men automatically urinate and every water trough was surrounded by pissing blokes.

We spent the afternoon exploring, sunbathing and waiting for our friends to turn up. When they did, in the early evening, we were standing in one of the tents wondering since when had Republica qualified as a dance act, let alone a good one. That was the signal to take some serious class As, and the experience really took off.

I've never taken so much speed before or since but somehow the occasion called for it. The numbers had been imperceptibly growing all day and now the event was jammed. The night passed with such a feeling of freedom and hedonism that there were no-holds-barred; it wasn't even comparable to the best buzz you get inside a club. The night was cold and people were lighting fires; you could see the stars and hear the wind in the trees and all around you were people who at that moment were thinking like you; had the same objectives as you; people who in the 'real world' you might not give the time of day but who would look out for you here; who you'd pass in the street without a glance but who were like family now; who had sober and responsible jobs and whole other lives and identities that at that time *didn't matter* because you were all here, in this place, with each other, to dance.

And dance we did. It was hard to fit in everyone you wanted to see, but I think I managed most on my list. We stood in silent (and slightly puzzled) tribute to Kraftwerk; danced like dervishes to the frenzied genius of Daft Punk (albeit constricted dervishes; you could hardly move in that tent when they came on and the lads who climbed the tent supports had the right idea); lost it completely to Faithless; and rounded it off in the morning by dancing madly in homage to Jeff Mills: a perfect end to an unbelievable night.

We saw other acts, and lots of other things happened that night (like the bloke who ODd on Charlie who we found barely breathing under a tree; who we managed after prolonged effort – and no help from the so-called medics – to bring round only to be told to *fuck off*. But now the whole weekend has begun to blur into one confused kaleidoscope of noise and colour.

But it's the feeling that remains true and clear. Going to a club is a severely diluted version of the same sense of togetherness and community. And if events like Tribal Gathering are only pale reflections of the illegal raves and free parties of the late eighties and early nineties, then I'll always be gutted I missed out.
Anon, London

I think it was in 1994 that I first discovered my own style of music, outside of the gay scene. Nowadays, I think that the gay scene is tired and uninspiring; everyone just wants to look the same and I'm fed up with it. Now I don't go out on the scene at all and I only work in straight clubs. In the beginning, when I was playing as part of the gay scene, I took over a role which had been established for a couple of years, and I had to change it to suit me – I didn't suit it. And that's where my choice of music came in, and that's where it started for me, when I went out on my own and found a different style which I hadn't heard anywhere else.

And I kind of realise now much more than I did then – I can look back clearly at what I was doing. I did invent a different sound, but not intentionally. I basically tailor-made a set for myself, and it became 'nu-energy'. I'm really proud of it now, because it's here to stay, and it's not a dirty word any more, which is cool. And the club got busier and busier, and my residency became permanent. And about six months later I gave an interview to a magazine in which my style was first called 'nu-energy'.
Blu Peter, DJ, London

Fenced in one huge field, the rave is enormous. Most are held in warehouses or disused aeroplane hangars but this one is totally open-air. People are milling around; dancing, smiling and shaking hands with everyone else. An earnest, balding young bloke dashes up and whispers into Max's ear, *Don't touch the mad yellow ones*, and zips away. A girl with sunglasses and bunches offers them cigarettes. *Please take them*, she says. *I've just given up. Please have them*. The relief of getting in somewhere coupled with the music, people and pharmaceuticals gradually working in their stomachs has compounded their intoxication of the scene. *Why is it girls always look gorgeous on E whilst blokes look like shit?* Max asks Ivan as they clump forward.

Swirling loved-up faces and the kick of the bass drum suck them closer to the music. A geezer in fluorescent green cycling shorts and a bright orange vest-top rocks to and fro to the beat. Confrontation with intense pounding rhythms causes a chemical reaction which triggers Sparkie off big time. Jacking his arms around exuberantly, he feels like someone has popped a cork on top of his head, letting a shower of glowing sensations burst out. He tries to smile at everyone, shake their hands and say hello. A well-built bloke in a bright yellow sweat-shirt dances hectically within a group of happy-looking friends. His arms fly around his head, making patterns and shapes to the music. Sparkie squeezes his way through to him.

God bless you and your team! he cries. The bloke pauses, a little confused, and answers in a thick Liverpudlian accent. *Err ... cheers ... what's your name?* Dizzily, Sparkie replies, *I'm not here.* The scouser laughs, *What are you on? Another planet,* Sparkie deadpans as he reels away, lured by the pumping sound.

Debbie stands awkwardly, nervously tapping her foot. She feels most peculiar. Warm, squelchy rushes rise within her. The sensation isn't unpleasant, she just doesn't know what to do with herself. Max asks Ivan whether he thinks Jim and their other friends will be here. Ivan shrugs his shoulders distantly. With a sharp intake of air he approaches Debbie and asks her if she wants to dance. Max reluctantly follows them, a pace behind.

A tingling sensation crawls up their bodies. They feel lighter as their hearts pump faster and bits of their bodies jerk to the beat.

Exchanging silent smiles, they all know that their drugs are nearly up. Around them, almost everyone in the field is dancing. Dancing is suddenly the only natural purpose in life, as if it would be alien to ever stop. A swollen mass of bobbing heads moves more intensely.

Unexpectedly, the infectious music drifts off to nothing. Cheers and whistles go up. The crowd look around dazed, waiting for something to happen. Max starts to panic that it's been raided already. A haze of smoke is pumped from a machine under the makeshift stage. A green laser cuts icily through it as soft piano chords pad up and down. Everyone recognises the tune instantly. The cheers and whistles reach a crescendo. The timing is amazing. Max, Ivan and Debbie suddenly lose control of their bodies as a sizzling rush burns up their spines to their heads. As a more strident string sound breaks in, the three of them spontaneously hug each other, grinning like buffoons. Everyone is hugging everyone, putting their hands in the air or shutting their eyes in rapture. When the jerking uproarious rhythm eventually breaks in, the whole crowd goes totally bananas. The sky explodes as the laser rips smoothly into the night and limbs flap wildly in every direction.

Mickey and Louise run excitedly over to them. They can tell they've come up as well. The five of them embrace, bouncing up and down in a cluster. A shared feeling of jubilant warmth flows through the group and they touch without traces of embarrassment or self-consciousness. A cushion of well-being protects them from the outside world. Between a sandwich of music, drugs and good friends, they have escaped the present and the mundane.

Daniel Newman, London

All material by Daniel Newman is taken from his novel Dance You Suckers *and although written in the second person is based on his own experiences and those of his friends.*

Energy, Shepherd's Bush film studios, 27 May 1989: This was the first full-on rave I ever went to. I'd heard about these big outdoor parties, but I didn't know what to expect. As I walked in I could see all these people standing on speakers chanting, *Mental, mental, radio rental* . . . and I'd heard about this chant and knew this was it, I was at a proper rave. They were all in their dungarees and pork-pie hats and beads and tie-dye, and half of them on acid as well as E, and you'd be forgiven for thinking the sixties had come around again, especially with the whole loved-up vibe that there was then.

Then I bumped into Graham Ball, who ran all the Westworld stuff – Enter the Dragon, Carwash, Joel's Exit – and I asked him what he thought of it. He said he thought it was really good, and asked if I'd been to the main room yet, where it was really going off. I'd only been in two rooms and the outside courtyard where the (deflated) bouncy castle was, and I'd thought that was it. So I entered this room and, to this day, I got more of a thrill walking into that room than from anything else I did after. There was a romanesque dance platform in the centre, with supporting pillars, almost like a temple, and the lasers were coming down around it, lighting up the people dancing on it, and the packed dancefloor, and the dancers on the wide ledge around the edge of the room.

Then, as I was standing there, taking in the sheer numbers of people, and the chanting, and the strange dancing with bizarre hand movements, I heard it. *Yeeeeeeees. Yeeeeeeees*, it went. *Live an' direct: a man like Adamskiii* . . . I couldn't work out where it was coming from at first. I hadn't even seen the stage. Then I saw the bloke standing at the keyboard, and the nutty-looking black guy with the dreads, dancing and chattering on in Jamaican patois, and when the music really kicked in the whole place just erupted. I mean it really went berserk. Everyone had been dancing anyway, but all of a sudden they were dancing that much faster, that much harder. I'd been smoking draw and doing coke all night, so I was pretty out of it, but I'd never done any E, and I turned to my brother Tim and said, *What the fuck are these people on?* and even as I asked it I knew the answer. And I resolved then and there that next time we went out I was going to do an E. From then on in, for the rest of that year and (as I thought at the time) for the foreseeable future I was out there, every weekend, living it, out of it.

Simon, London

The first time I DJd for the public was in Luton. I was working as a barman in a club and the DJ got too pissed to play his set. The guy who owned the club turned around to me and said,

You've got some records with you, why don't you do a set? *The first record I played was my favourite record, but it didn't turn out too well and everyone left the dancefloor, I mean everyone! So I put on something different and brought them back, and the next one kept them there, and I realised then that I was hooked; watching people dancing and knowing I'm the one that picks them up . . .*

Now I've got a regular slot in London and I'm building that up; more and more people are coming and it's gradually getting more and more well-known, so I'm getting more money to buy even more records and play better and better sets. Who knows where it will lead.
Leeroy, Luton

I stood there, shocked, distraught. I couldn't believe the sight that stared back at me through the crystal clarity of the mirror. The same man who had, only twenty-four hours before, been the Indie kid that I had grown to respect and even admire. The same man who had listened to the lifeless music and nonsensical lyrics, and pondered over the adorning stardom of its tedious musicians. The same man who had never heard of club legends such as Carl Cox, Sasha or Paul Oakenfold. A man for whom life had not yet begun.

And now, that man had gone, ten years of life wiped clean in one single night.

Good riddance.

The image reflected was a complete wreck, someone barely recognisable as myself, someone I had never seen before. The image was dreadful but it could never reflect how I felt because I was a great deal worse. I felt like the blue piece of fluff in a fat man's bellybutton.

My pupils were wide like a day-dead trout and the glaze which shrouded them was as thick as any fog. They rebelled against the light that streamed in through the window, and yearned for the darkness once more, wanting to be back in the night and back at Cream in Liverpool. They wanted to witness again the beautiful crowd, watch the surge of energy roll over the venue as the massive tunes were slammed. They needed to again stand amongst them and be part of them, pumping arms and legs to the addictive beat. And more than anything they wanted to watch the man at the centre, crouched over, controlling the decks like a master. They wanted to be part of his party and rise and fall with his awesome presence.

My ears were still ringing from the head-splitting sounds that had swept me away. A wall of sound that had been selected and unleashed by an absolute genius. They were numb from the words of my friend, Smiler, ushering the godlike name of Carl Cox, a man I had never heard of, let alone seen. The man who had stood just a few feet away and smiled along with the elated crowd. Carl Cox, the man, the god, whose name I would never forget.

I moved my jaw and felt it unhinge away from my fur-lined teeth. It was incredibly stiff, locked from the two packs of chewing gum and half my tongue that I'd eaten through the night. I eventually stripped the swollen chunk of muscle that had once passed as a tongue from its sweaty retreat glued against the roof of my mouth and found a taste that I had previously not uncovered. I looked back towards the bedroom half expecting to find the cat that had pissed within my gaping orifice.

I took a breath through my mouth and felt it grate down my arid throat. I dared not gasp through my nose and the passage is now redundant to me. It is now owned by the spidery black substance that dwells there, lurking in the cavity and spreading its legs to encompass my whole head, capturing the thoughts that barely register.

I looked down at the redundant skin that hung over the weary jut of my ribcage and rubbed a hand over it. A question hits me, *Where the fuck had I been last night?* I couldn't remember even laying a hand to the floor so where the hell had the shit that covered every fingernail come from?

The question spun me out and sent me reeling backwards. I looked down at the toothbrush in the vague knowledge that I had to do something with it in order to get my teeth cleaned. The heavy thoughts came and went one by one but never stayed, leaving me with the feeling of breathing through a worn sock. I felt shagged. I just wanted to hit the sack, disappear from the sight of my parents and crawl back into my little hole. But I couldn't do that. I had to make a move or they would suspect. Come up to check like the loving family they are.

I turned towards the toilet just for the relief of not having to look at myself. I lifted the seat and stared into the white porcelain at the bottom of the bowl while I figured out what to do next. I eventually remembered and went to grab the little fella, only that little fella ain't my little fella, he was a lot fucking bigger when I left last night. My little fella was soft and floppy while this one was like a broken matchstick: small, hard and extremely wooden. Maybe mine stayed in the club, not daring to leave, jiving his little end away with the rest of the crowd. Maybe I'd got someone else's. *No, not possible*, I told myself with a smile. I never saw any five-year-olds in there.

I forced out a piss, which was extremely difficult. It felt like my stomach was gonna explode before the pelvic muscle relented. I attained a short-lived success and was met with a slow dribble which felt like pissing battery acid. I let out a gasp but it was too late, realising that once the pelvic muscle is open it's not too keen on closing again. I glared at the burning dribble of Irn-bru that turned the bowl a bright orange on contact. *Fucking hell*, I whispered in shock as the liquid slowed to a trickle.

I turned to the mirror and looked at the shocked expression that glared back at me. I'm bewildered at first but the drawn features of my face quickly turn to mild surprise. The night finally registered in the dim corner of my mind and a thousand images come flooding back. A wave of goose-pimples crawled over every inch of my body and settled on my face, spreading an outlandish grin of joy.

What a fucking night, I said to myself in euphoria and instantly realised that there was no looking back for this dance freak.

Jack Woffenden, Barnsley

Before he left, my dad was always trying to stop the two of us ever having fun, ever going out. Just because he was the man, he thought he ruled the house. It was more like because he had a shitty job, had drunk his whole life away at forty, and was jealous of us that he treated us like shit. Still, when he wanted to, he had a wicked sense of humour, could have us in stitches. We'd be walking down the street, and he'd see a woman looking for something on the ground, and he'd say: *She's wondering where her life's gone.* Only that was just a flash of what he must've been like when he was younger. Bitter, that's him. Bitter, and angry. Frustrated. All the worst cancers. And so that affects me. Why the fuck would I want to stay around the house when he's around, on the settee, belly hanging out, fag in hand, grabbing for more beer when he's just spent all night in the pub, or out, boozing at work? Fuck that. So when I started staying over at friends' houses, just to get away from him and actually enjoy my life, he started ringing me, drunk, telling me to get home; and when I wouldn't, he'd wait till the next day, and lay into me, screaming and shouting, *You're only fourteen years old! Stay in with your fucking mother for Christ's sake!*

When he hit me that was it. My mum started crying and told him to go, to get out. *How the hell can you hit your own daughter!* she shouted at him as he staggered there, drunk, watching me cry.

So he went.

That was last week. Tonight's Saturday night, and I'm here at the club, all glammed up, loads of make-up on. The bouncers didn't even think about my age when I walked past them; they were too busy winking at me. They obviously didn't know who I was.

Here comes my mum with the drinks. Water of course. You have to drink water if you want Es to work properly, that's what the woman who we got them off said. I never realised women sold drugs. I thought it was just men.

Here you go says my mum, giving me a bottle of water. She looks worried. *Feel anything yet love?* I dunno, Mum I reply. *My arms feel a little tingly, but that might just be the lights and the music. What about you? I'm not sure either* she says. *I tell you what though, no one's even looked at me funny yet. I thought all the young 'uns would be wondering what an old woman like me was doing out. Don't be silly, Mum,* I say.

Now I can feel it, something's rising in my legs, something like a sudden load of butterflies in my stomach and I look up at my mum, and she's got this look on her face, like she's seeing and feeling something she's not used to. It's a look of wonder, and she grabs my hand and it feels warm, it feels so warm . . .

My God! My God! Can you feel it, it's mad! I feel so . . . Suddenly she's clinging to me, and I'm clinging to her, hard, neither of us can speak, it's mad! The lights and the music and the people around are blurring. Whatever's inside is touching us both all over. We know it because it's in our eyes. We can speak through them, telepathy, and somehow we're kind of rising above the club, though we're still stood on the spot, and now inside, we feel warm, relaxed, good, so good, it's unbelievable.

My God, love! Can you believe it! I can't believe it! This is wonderful! Everything seems so good, she cries, taking a look round. *It all seems so . . . so . . . pure. Oh just let me stroke your hands, oh they're so lovely, you look so beautiful darling. So do you, Mum* I reply, gazing at her. *Your eyes, they're so kind, you, you're so kind! There's like an aura coming from you. It seems like it's flowing between us! Can you feel it? Oh yes love, oh yes* she says. *My God what is this feeling! It's like . . . I'm in love all over again. What a feeling . . . I'm so glad we came! I just can't believe it! What it does to you! . . . I shouldn't even be here, but taking an Ecstasy! Both of us together! I can't believe it! . . . I'm so glad we came. My God can you feel it?! Jesus Christ! Give us a hug darling!*

And as the E floods us with its magic, we hug, feeling the music and the people and the sheer love rising up us, as we burst into tears of joy.
Jamie Jackson, London

I had my first E experience when I was twenty-five, just a couple of years ago. It has led to many personal and spiritual experiences which have changed my life for the better. I thought at the time that I was pretty sorted and that I had a balanced view of the world, but I soon came to realise how much my own fears, prejudices and inhibitions were affecting the experiences I had in life.

I can remember that first time watching people bonding on and off the dancefloor, watching friends and strangers embrace, and I felt amazed and elated, and thought how right it seemed. A stranger caught my smile, and instead of stonewalling me, he smiled right back, and at that moment I felt my natural love for others bubble up as I lost my barriers of fear. I found that night that I was able to tell my friends how much I loved and valued them, and I could make connections with many other people because I had lost my usual mistrust of strangers. I remember also that night that I felt totally accepted as I was, and I could accept others in the same way – without prejudice clouding my perception.

I took that experience away from the club with me, and I found that I was liberated by this sudden loss of barriers. I learned that people respond positively to a projection of openness and trust, and negatively to fear and mistrust; and I saw clearly the influences of these energies within the universe.

I knew some of this before of course; I knew that a smile could be infectious, and I understood the principles of projecting good or bad vibes, but ecstasy showed me how things could be when we *all* feel safe and unthreatened, when we *all* feel accepted and loved.

I have had many beautiful and fulfilling experiences since then, some on E and some not; but each one of them because I have replaced fear with trust, and hate with love. I have deepened all of my personal relationships through expressing my true feelings of love and friendship, and I am able to do this because I know now that I am not somehow lessening myself by doing so, rather that I am contributing to a positive love energy which benefits us all.

Tanya, South London

The first time I took ecstasy was at the Hacienda, at a night called Nude. It was 1989 and I was in my thirties. I'd been in the army for years and I'd never taken any illicit substances and when I came out I wondered, *What's going on here then?* My friends explained what was happening and I thought, *Go on then, I'll have some of that.* I didn't do it straight away, though. First, I bought some books and read up on the subject and decided I'd have a go.

That first time I did only a quarter of an E and it totally wasted me. I did half a trip, too, and I'd never done acid before either. I didn't know who I was, where I was, or why I was there anyway!

It was a totally warm sensation, a sensation of well-being, euphoria, with no barriers, unlimited love for everyone and everything around me and a feeling of total elation. They were playing early house music. Li'l Louis Vega doing 'French Kiss', Graeme Park, Wilson ... I was converted.

From then on I started going clubbing every weekend. We'd go to Shelley's Laserdome in Stoke-on-Trent to see Sacha, to the Eclipse in Coventry ... wherever we knew would be a good night. You could get pure MDMA capsules in those days and half a capsule would make you totally faced for nine or ten hours. It was amazing.

I don't think we'll ever get back to what it was like in those days. It was all new then and you can never regain the past. The inception of the Criminal Justice Bill has changed a lot too; I think that the days of the large raves are numbered because now it's all about money.

But the scene itself won't ever end; it's just changing.
Anon, Birmingham

moments of madness

It was in 1989 at Sin at the Astoria. The place was full and I had the job of cueing the DJs and introducing the guests on to the stage. I was backstage with one of my friends, Kevin, and we were laughing and joking and buzzing, as one does, and the crowd was all dancing and whilst I was waiting to go on he bet me that I wouldn't go on naked. I thought to myself that there was no way I was going to do that, but he says, *Go on, I bet you £20.*

It was a spur-of-the-moment decision. As I walked on to the stage, Nicky Holloway thought I was coming on to introduce the PA and started going, *One, two . . . one, two . . .* on the mike. It wasn't until I got to the centre of the stage that he realised I'd got no clothes on, and he was literally lost for words.

Everyone was looking. The place was packed and it took two thousand people. I calmly took a bow, smiled and walked off the stage without saying anything. When I got off the stage, my mate Kevin couldn't talk for three-quarters of an hour and he looked like his face was going to burst, he was laughing so much!

Afterwards, I couldn't believe I'd done it. But I'd got my £20.
Dillon, London

The funniest thing I can remember happening didn't happen at a club but afterwards.

Me and my mates Gary, Paul, Simon (little) and Simon (large) had been out to a club in Bristol and we were walking home at the crack of dawn to the house I shared with Paul. It was freezing and we were walking fast, heads down, concentrating on getting back to the warm flat and having a spliff. It had been a blinding night of drum and bass madness and we had been off our faces all night. We'd got pissed before we got there and then had pills and Billy, no wonder we weren't feeling too clever. You know when your legs feel empty and your joints feel tender, not painful yet but you know they will be. You're still rushing off the speed and so you're concentrating very hard and you still feel alert but you also feel fucked. And you know that the alert bit will decrease and the fucked bit increase and you don't want to be outside in the cold when this is happening, you want to be inside with a spliff and a cup of tea.

So we were walking along, and to get back to mine you have to go through a car park of a supermarket. It's one of the big ones, I won't say which! We got halfway across the car park when we heard it: *HELLO!* came a big booming voice. We stopped in our tracks. It must have looked quite funny, we just froze mid-step.

Cautiously, we looked around. There was no one in any direction, just a frosty, deserted car park. Gary took a step back on to his back foot: we all did. *HELLO!* it went again. We looked at each other. Gary (who must have twigged what was happening) began bouncing up and down, a big grin spreading across his face. *HELLO! I'M A SPECIAL PARKING SPACE FOR DISABLED PEOPLE!* it boomed. We had somehow activated the sensor on a parking space by walking over it! We were all jumping up and down now! *DO YOU REALLY NEED TO USE*

ME? IF NOT, PLEASE PARK ELSEWHERE! IF YOU NEED ANYTHING, JUST ASK! and then it played a jingle!

And it was the jingle that really did it for us. When you've been out of your face for hours and hours in a club with deafening drum and bass pounding through your body, and you're suddenly outside in the silence with your ears ringing and your voice fucked, you crave music of any kind, you can still hear the beat, your mind is convinced it can still hear it anyway. You hear rhythms in your footsteps, in passing cars, anything. And here we had found something that played a jingle! A crappy one like on *Hi-De-Hi*, but it was still music to our ears. We knew what we had to do.

There was nothing we could do about the words bit that came before the jingle, but Simon and Simon went on to the next parking space and between them they set that one off. Before long we had worked it out so that by jumping backwards and forwards they made the first bit of *HELLO!* repeat over and over (sort of) in time, like a bass, and me and Gary and Paul had the jingle bit going on the other one, over the top, like a tune!

We must have looked mad. It was freezing cold, crack of dawn, and here we were in a deserted car park jumping up and down, off our faces, convinced we were making music! We'd completely forgotten about the nice warm house and the spliff and the tea. We'd all come up again on the adrenalin anyway.

We made it back to the house eventually, tearing ourselves away from our music. But it still lays us out when we think of what we must have looked like, our makeshift crappy 'tune' booming forth across the car park!

Andy, Swansea

We'd gone with only a bag of whizz, expecting it to be easy to score the other goodies there. Wrong. V97 was dry. Finally, a chance meeting with a 'glazed over'-looking guy in the car park had our pockets full of space invader acid and dollar pills. A pill was gobbled immediately and off we happily bumbled to the dance tent to get ourselves settled to watch Dreadzone. You know when you've got that 'happiest moment of my life' feeling? This was one of those times – good pills! So down with the acid.

The acid lately has been pretty poor quality, so I didn't expect the head charge that I gratefully received. I knew things were getting pretty mad when Andy had to explain toilet etiquette to me – little things like hitch up skirt and pull down knickers before urinating! It took some explaining. But it wasn't long before I'd forgotten that I'd ever wanted to piss. I was getting a real feeling that I needed to be taken away from society. So we weaved and floated our way out of the dance tent and across the field.

Things at this point started to get very tricky. We found the way out, but to leave from this exit point you went up eight steps, walked across a small platform, and down another eight steps to get out. We reached the steps, I went up the first three, when it suddenly became clear to me that I was being ushered on to the stage to do a live spot alongside the headlining band, Blur. Elation set in, then comical horror – what was I going to sing? Would I walk right past the band on stage because I didn't have a clue what Blur looked like? Did I look a mess? God, couldn't they see I was just some tripped-out fucker? All these thoughts were running around my head, but I could definitely see them clearing the space to lead me on stage. The crowd were cheering. I grabbed a security guard: *You've made a mistake, you've made a mistake*! I pleaded with him. By now the other half of me was getting geared up for my fifteen minutes of fame. Then it really did become clear to me – Blur were playing, but a quarter of a mile away at the other end of the field! I glanced up towards Andy. He knew exactly what I'd been experiencing. *You thought you were going on stage with Blur*, he said through his grinning smile.

He made a decision that I should be taken away from there. He led me up the rest of the steps, across the platform and down the other side of the steps, only to find that we'd picked the wrong exit point and were now in amongst the thousands of hardcore Blur fans. Hysterical laughter was creeping in, my head was getting messy and I was laughingly trying to apologise to the Blur fans. When I realised that it was a wasted mission, I decided I should go back and explain to the security guard that I was just a bit messy at the moment and apologise for any inconvenience caused. Andy took a firm hold and finally got me out of there.

D. Day, Nottingham

I used to dress up like Andy Pandy when I went out. I had an Andy Pandy suit tailor-made by a proper tailor with the silly hat and the stripes, and I used to dance on stage, just for a laugh. And on the back of my Andy Pandy suit were two words: FUCKIN' FUCKIT. I danced with the Prodigy at a Perception party in Oxford, at Quest in Wolverhampton, the Eclipse . . . I got well-known for it. Everyone used to recognise me.

Another time I went out clubbing as Mickey Mouse – the full head and ears and everything. We were on the way to the club in the car and we were all dressed up – we had a French tart, a Harem girl, a skeleton and a naughty nurse in the car, and I was driving with the Mickey head on. We must have freaked out every straight person on the motorway!
Ralf E. P. (Oracle), Birmingham

It was the New Year of 1990–91 and, as usual, myself and my mates were skint after Christmas. This year we had heard that there was to be a free New Year jam at the Roundhouse in Camden. We were told that it was to be a kind of crusty/psychedelic/rave type thang. Normally I wouldn't be down for this as I like my beats funky, but with having less money than a blind Maxwell pensioner at a poker game, I decided it would be the best option. As long as we had enough shit to smoke, snort or swallow, who gave a fuck where you were, right?!!

For those who don't know it, the Roundhouse is a large, old engine shed. It is circular and has a conical roof with a balcony running around the outside edge supported by numerous pillars. It was used in the late sixties as a venue for various acid freak-outs with the likes of Jefferson Airplane, The Doors and The Who playing there, but for years it had lain empty after aborted attempts to use it as a theatre, amongst other things. It had recently been occupied by a load of travellers and they were regularly holding raves there.

It's a fairly disorientating venue at the best of times, but on this occasion it was just plain fucking insane! It was almost pitch-black inside save for one or two low-powered spotlights placed in the centre of the black void. I would estimate there were probably around 2,300–3,000 people inside, all in various stages of chemical intoxication. Some kind of PA had been erected but it was far too weak to fill the space or combat the sound of fireworks being let off inside. Some crazy bastards were firing rockets and throwing bangers off the balcony circling us overhead. I was just waiting for some poor acid casualty to get taken out by a blast of gunpowder. At one point two police officers walked in through the crowd straight through the middle of the heaving mass of ravers, dreads, freaks, fags and other assorted bug-eyed goons. As they pushed their way through they were illuminated by a spotlight tracking them as they went. Within seconds there was a cacophony of boos, jeers and obscenities. To this day I don't know where they ended up, as they just seemed to melt into the darkness at the other side of the building.

We dropped our pills – New Yorkers or Callies, I really can't remember. I never have been one of those people who fetishise the names of every drug known to man like some kind of walking pharmacopoeia. We waited for the New Year to arrive. There was no announcement as to the time and so we didn't know when we had left 1990 and entered 1991. We didn't care though. We just tried to make the best of the terrible PA. In fact, I don't think there was even a DJ, as we soon noticed that the same three or four tracks were being played again and again in the same order as though on some kind of tape. Either that or the DJ had lost his wax in the vacuum of blackness that was the Roundhouse that night.

At some point, I don't know how or when, myself and Keith were separated from the other three guys. By this time our pills had kicked in and someone had lit a bonfire in the middle of the building. At least now there was a modicum of light. It was at this point that things started to get very weird. I mean very weird indeed, in a kind of David-Lynch-fucked-up-Jacob's-Ladder type of way. All I remember is that I woke suddenly out of some kind of trance. I was suddenly aware of where I was and, in doing so, realised that I had previously been totally disconnected from everything in or around me. I don't know how long I had been in this kind of limbic state, it could have been a minute or it could have been an hour. All I know is that when I came to I was standing in the Roundhouse feeling aware that I had just been unaware. Check it? In all the times that I took acid – and I had taken some heavy shit – I had been lucky never to have had an even vaguely unpleasant experience. Similarly with Es. This time, however, I stood there trying to work out where the fuck my mind had been before I had come back to reality (of sorts!). As I attempted to work out what was happening inside my head, I reassured myself by saying, *OK, man. Don't get paranoid* . . .

Shit!!! As soon as I said that word I was fucked. I could feel the panic level in me rise at an exponential rate. Every nanosecond, every tiny moment in time, I was aware of the rapid increase in my unusual state. At no point was I actually scared. In essence, I was more fascinated by what was happening to me. I was extremely aware of my thought processes in all their multiplex levels of operation, and it seemed like millions. All the time this was happening I managed to retain a rational, analytic portion of my mind which literally kept my feet on the ground. At times, however, I got to the point of having to remind myself of my exact location in the universe! What I mean is, there were occasions when I had totally no idea of where I was in time or space. So I had to remind myself in a methodical manner along the lines of, *OK, you're in 1991, in the universe, in the Milky Way, the solar system, the earth, Britain, London, Camden, Roundhouse, HERE!!* This process of location was accompanied by an internal visualisation like a lens rapidly zooming in from outer space down through the planets to earth and finally down to where I was at that moment. I know it sounds fucking crazy and it was, but I had to do it. All of this took place in a period of about ten to fifteen seconds. It was a very rapid process and one I was aware of at every single moment in time.

At this point, I decided to ask my friend Keith if he was feeling all right, hoping that I wasn't the only one experiencing apparent ontological collapse. When he said that he too was feeling very odd, I felt a wave of relief, not through any kind of schadenfreude, but through the kind of comfort found in a shared community of experience. In this case, losing it big time in a virtually pitch-black cavern full of tripping goons. Keith and I had lost the other three, and we decided to move closer to the bonfire in the centre of the building. So, like some shaman in a Peyote-induced trance, we guided each other over to the edge of the bonfire to join the others gazing into its glowing tendrils. The dancing fire swept up into the darkness of the Roundhouse and played ghostly patterns over the faces of those assembled around it. The orange flickering effect seemed to heighten the already acid-like warping of people's features which my frying brain was trying to make intelligible. As we stood vacantly drying our eyeballs by the fire, through the flames, on the other side, both of us caught sight of a freaky-looking dude who must of stood about five feet high and had a remarkable resemblance to Catweazel, that hippy-trippy tramp-cum-wizard from the seventies' TV series. As soon as we had clocked him, we both knew that he would come around to us and, fuck me, he did! We stood rooted to the spot as he fixed his little black eyes on us and slowly navigated the edge of the bonfire to come and stand right next to us. He finally ended up next to me chatting to someone and, from what I could hear of the conversation, he had a voice that was more camp than a row of tents. It was just bugged-out shit!!

After I don't know how long, we decided to try and find the others and went off in search. It was at this time that a new phenomenon was experienced by us. This can be best described as a kind of quasi-translocation experience! That's to say, you know when you're in a club and the place where you are dancing becomes familiar to you through its relative position to the rest of the club and through recognising others around you? Well, a kind of translocation occurs when, after feeling sure you recognise all around you and you have your bearings, you move only a matter of a few feet and the effect is as if you have moved to the other side of the club. Well, check this. On this night, my translocation was a *mutha!* I only had to step a few fucking inches, man, and it was as if I had been shot not to the other side of the building but to the other side of the freaking Milky Way. I mean, I would take a step and suddenly the place where I had been for a few minutes was now inhabited by completely different people. I could not recognise a single aspect of where I had been just a moment ago. The circular design of the Roundhouse didn't help either, with no flat walls to get any bearings.

If that wasn't enough, I began to experience the most acute aural distortions I have ever known. In fact, aural hallucinations would be a more accurate description. Voices were mutated and twisted in such a way as to make them sound completely unintelligible, save for every third or fourth word which, to my ears anyway, seemed to be either my name or a comment on some aspect of my dancing! This was obviously Captain Paranoia starting to call the shots. It was only this element that I truly found disturbing. My man Keith described it best when he said that he too had aural disturbances and said it sounded like 'robotic Swedish', like some sort of vocoder shit going down from a Zapp album – only in Swedish!! Sort of like, *Zzzzwwwweeerrhh bbrrrruuuup look at him zzzeeepprrruuupp bbwwwuuuurreeepp!!* It was totally flipped-out shit! Initially, we thought our Es had been dosed with a generous dash of heavy acid. We still don't know exactly what made us trip out like that. The other guys had the same Es as us but didn't get all the freaky shit going down like we did. All we can think now is that the Es reacted in some way with the skunk we were smoking because the others didn't have any. Anyway, Keith and I decided to leave after not being able to find the others.

Every time I was convinced I had seen one of them, I would go up to them and, just as I got to within a foot or so of them, the face I truly believed I'd recognised suddenly metamorphosed into the visage of some stranger. That happened about five or six times and so, thinking I had sustained some permanent genetic or neurological damage, we left the Roundhouse, stepping out of the darkness into the grey dawn of 1991. It was the oddest experience of our lives. Our journey on foot from Chalk Farm to Waterloo was a mental trek too, what with being accompanied by a pissed-up, totally indecipherable Glaswegian and meeting the universe's biggest bullshitting raver at the station – who Keith christened Top Boy Tim. But that's another pile of roaches.

Ramu, London

Conversation in the toilet:

What I want to know is this: how do we know how long to look at something?

You what?

Well, if you go to an art gallery and look at a painting, how long?

What the fuck are you on about? I don't fuckin' know!

But you do, and that's the point. Like if you stop in the park and look at the ducks, you might stop for say five minutes, and then start walking again, yeah . . .? But why?

I dunno, but I tell you what: remind me never to go walking with you in a fuckin' park. In fact, remind me never to go anywhere with you, especially not fuckin' raving and fuckin' clubbing 'cos you're doing my fuckin' head in! OK?!

Yeah, I suppose . . . but why is your head done in?
Jamie Jackson, London

In the old days, the legal clubs used to shut at three o'clock; there weren't any late-nighters. But if you knew the circuit, you could go to the illegal places like Clink Street, MethodAir, until about five in the morning and then what we used to do is get a cab down to London Bridge and go to Borough Market and drink in the market pubs because they were the only place you could get a drink at that time in the morning. They'd open at six for the stallholders and delivery drivers and market men, and we'd all pile in, the drag queens with all their make-up on, all the die-hards . . . the regulars didn't know what had hit them. It was bizarre. In the end it became a regular thing and everyone knew each other down there.

Dillon, London

Karma Sutra happened out of the blue. We'd meant to go to a Labyrinth event, down in the East End, but it was a bit dark and moody for us. We heard on Centre Force Radio that Karma Sutra was going off down in Kent, and we took off, following the directions on the radio. It was in marquees and circus tents; not too big, a real pukka do. The police presence was small, and it was a safe crowd. We got in eventually, and one of the first things we saw was a fairground they had set up, with a centrifuge. You had no worries about coming up on your E with one of them! But it must have been the middle of the night when I suddenly heard the DJ say *Look everyone! Look at that! Just look at those bloody idiots!* We looked where he was pointing and saw that a bunch of guys had got into the centrifuge, which is shaped like a drum and spins very fast on its side, and had got outside of the straps and were hanging on with their feet and hands, some of them upside down. They were off their faces, and I don't know if it was the same guys on it all night, but every time I looked, they were still there.

The police at Karma Sutra were sound. When we left, we were sitting in a queue of cars, and I could see this copper coming down the queue, leaning into every car and asking the driver questions. I still had various substances on me, and was just beginning to get a little paranoid when he got to us. *Morning!* he said . . . *Morning,* we replied. *Had a good night? he asked. Money well spent? Yeah, great . . .* we said. *Good, good; have a safe journey home now,* he said, before moving on to the next car. There was another copper who you would swear had been at the do all night, on a totally top buzz, and had just had time to go home and change into his uniform. We asked him the way back to London. *That way, mate,* he says, *or is it that way,* waving his arms about and gurning.

We heard later that the organiser of Karma Sutra actually ran out with all the money; the tent-hire people didn't get paid, the DJs didn't get paid; the security got paid because they were in it with the organiser. It was sad to hear about what actually went on behind the scenes; Karma Sutra was a safe event, and we knew then that there wouldn't be another.
Anon

I remember one rave I went to in Hull. I was still a student at the time and for some reason or other I had a free house. I'd said to my mates that they could all come back to mine afterwards and not long after we got there I could see one of my friends talking to some bloke he'd met, gesturing and pointing at me. It was obvious he was inviting him back to my house, but I wasn't bothered. The more the merrier, I thought.

But as the night went on I could see it happening more and more; my friends telling people they'd be welcome at my house afterwards. I wasn't sure whether it was my own paranoia but it began to seem as if everyone at the entire rave was going back to my place!

When morning came and it was time to leave, my mates and I began trudging towards the car. But every few steps we were stopped by some stranger asking for directions or telling us they'd see us in a bit and they'd just follow us back! I put my head down and tried to remain invisible to the hordes of people who'd been told there was something going off in Stockton and to follow me.

But just before we got to the car we had to pass a coach and that was when it really hit me; looking up at the coach we could see the windows were lined with gurning faces pressed against the glass giving us the thumbs-up, waving and gesturing! We were going to have to lose an entire coach!

The journey back was one I won't forget in a hurry. The coach remained stubbornly behind us for the entire length of the motorway, despite the cunning lane-changing tactics of our driver. We finally lost it on some B-road in the middle of nowhere and made it back to the house, paranoid, exhausted, but alone.

Paul, Stockton-on-Tees

I remember one mad thing we did once at the Hacienda back in 1989: *we got the little night-lights people use when fishing – like the glow sticks you see now but tiny. You had to break them in the middle to release the phosphorous and we got some of them and put them in our mouths, and at one point me and my friend Charlie were up on the stage, dancing and going mental, and all of a sudden Graeme Parks who was DJing started signalling us to go up to the DJ booth. We eventually got up there and it turned out he just wanted to know what the fuck we'd got in our mouths! Every time we laughed or spoke this eerie green glow was coming out of our mouths and no one could work out what it was.*

Ralf E. P. (Oracle), Birmingham

moments of madness

My mate Alan had turned up with a bag of almonds, determined he was going to give them out to people. This was at a Sunrise do at White Waltham. *Here mate, have an almond!* he went around saying. *Cheers mate! Nice one!* they all said, taking one. But can you think of anything worse to eat when you're off your head on E than an almond? Before long the place was full of people looking well unhappy, spitting out almonds, reaching for some water . . .

But he topped that when he discovered his penny whistle, which he insisted on calling a flute. He would go up to people, real close, and blow this thing tunelessly in their face. I got sick of people coming up to me, saying to me, *Your mate with the whistle – he's a real buzz-killer* . . .

Another mate, Nick, told us when we met up after an Energy event at Heston that he'd been hit, twice. Now we know Nick, and we know he gets on a bit of a mad one, so we asked him what he'd been doing at the time. *I found a cold water tap,* he said, *and it was free, so I was filling up my Evian bottle and throwing water over people to cool them down. And you know what?* he says. *A lot of people thought this was a really good idea. But I did it to this black guy and he fucking decked me!* The black guy had been watching Nick throwing water at people, seen him get closer and closer, probably thinking, *If that fucker comes anywhere near me . . .* which Nick eventually did, totally drenching him and getting decked. And so he's lying there on the ground, buzzing off four trips, going, *I'm sorry man, I'm sorry, please don't kill me, I'll never, ever do it again . . .*

And it's only a matter of hours before he gets decked again. *What were you doing this time?* we asked him. *Nothing!* he says, *Just dancing. On your own?* we asked. *No . . . next to some big geezer,* he says. *How close?* we asked. *Pretty close . . .* says Nick . . .
Simon, London

Although I've been going to clubs for years and immersed myself in the whole culture that surrounds it, one of the most immediate experiences that I've enjoyed most was the Autechre/Locust/ Seefeel/Mu-Ziq gig at the London Astoria 2 on 23 March 1994. As soon as I heard about it I rushed out to buy tickets, as these were probably the most talked-about acts at the time, and needless to say expectations were high. As we walked in the DJ was playing some funky techno and setting the mood nicely. First off was Locust, although I had never heard his music before and it was a dark ambient/techno hybrid which gave me an acid flashback halfway through the set! Then next was Autechre who just tore it up with their style, but during their set this girl comes up to me and says, *Excuse me, but isn't your name Mike? No,* I say, so she walks off and I don't think any more of it and carry on dancing to Autechre. About half an hour after their set, as I'm going upstairs to the bar, coming down the other way is one of the blokes from Autechre. He looks at me and says, *Mike, Mike, Richard wants to see you backstage,* then he gets a closer look. *Sorry mate, I thought you was someone else,* and scampers off.

So by now I'm getting puzzled and wondering what the bloody hell's going on. Seefeel were on next and did their dub/guitar thing; Richard James (Aphex Twin) was on the decks before Mu-Ziq came on, and doing a fine job he was too. But as I'm dancing away, I glance over to the stage and see this bloke setting some equipment up, and I take another glance and just stop dead in my tracks as I start to realise what's going on. Mike Parandinas who is half of Mu-Ziq, looks exactly like me and we are dressed exactly the same! Long hair, glasses, skinny and dressed all in black! Although my girlfriend at the time pointed out that he's quite a bit shorter than me, apart from that we were dead ringers. After Richard James finishes his set, Mu-Ziq start off with the first track from their album (this was apparently their first live gig and they had not long released their first album, *Tango 'n' Vectif* which was and still is absolutely blinding). The set was really tearing but as I'm down the front jigging away, there's loads of people looking at me and then Mike and giving me some really strange looks like I'm some kind of perverted groupie or something! Some remark was made to my girlfriend about me being his brother and I'm finding all this really quite funny. After the set, I'm upstairs having a drink and about four people come up and congratulate me on a wicked set, on which I told them that I wasn't Mike, although I could have bullshitted my way through!

It was a top night with the vibe and the music. That alone would have been enough to have made it memorable, but the Mike Parandinas comparison on top was definitely the funniest thing I've ever experienced on a night out.

Incidentally, just over a year later I was working in a local record shop when Mike Parandinas walks in! It turns out that he only lives down the road from me with his girlfriend. He remembered the night at the Astoria 2 and he told me that I actually put him off! I still see him from time to time and say hello.

Tony Scopes, East London

This happened at a warehouse rave in Plumstead back in 1992. There was one boy in particular (who we christened The Ketamine Kid) who was properly mashed up – he was looking over his shoulder and going, *Ssh, ssh, they'll see you*, and, *Ssh, be quiet*. I clocked he had an invisible friend and creased up; me and my friend Lloyd sat next to him for a while just watching. Suddenly I just knew what I had to do. I started going, *Oh, no,* *shit, where is it?* and searching where I'd been sitting. Lloyd stared at me and I winked at him. *Help me look for it, c'mon.* He started looking around him and I acted more and more frantic, attracting everybody's attention. I could feel The Ketamine Kid noticing me and I motioned him over; he looked scared but started bouncing over as Karen and Darren were going, *Yeah, yeah, please help us, please.* I was biting my lip so hard trying not to laugh, but it was difficult. *Please, please, help us,* I said. The Ketamine Kid was looking suspicious but despite himself intrigued. Lloyd and me were babbling at him, *Only you can help us, please help us.* He nodded vaguely as everyone gathered round us and I grabbed Lloyd's hand, waving it in The Ketamine Kid's face screaming, *Oh God, please help us. He's lost his fingers* . . . because you see Lloyd *had* lost two fingers in an industrial accident years ago, and he's going to The Ketamine Kid, *Yeah mate, I've dropped them somewhere, will you give me a hand finding them?*

The Ketamine Kid totally, utterly, absolutely lost the plot. It was like watching someone's brain spontaneously combust. He started screaming, *Nooo, nooo, there's five. Look: one, two, three, four, five. No, noo!* He just refused to accept there weren't five fingers. He was grabbing Lloyd's hand and going, *See, see, there's five, no, no, there* is, *there* is. We were crying with laughter, falling around on top of each other. I nearly wet myself, I was laughing so hard. The Ketamine Kid bounced out screaming, *Aaah, aaah, aaah, I'm not mad, I'm not, I'm not,* which made us laugh even more.

Kate Ferrie, London

Some mad geezer had come up to me and given me a sheet of thirty trips, told me to look after them for him, he'd be back for them later. You know how it was back in them mad days. Well I looked after them; started handing them out free to anyone I saw who looked like they needed one. It was later on, I was looking at this nutter, running around outside the building, looked like he was pretending to drive a car. Operating the steering-wheel, gearbox, making engine noises. Another bloke was looking at him too; I caught his eye and went over to chat with him. *See that geezer, he's mad, he thinks he's a car,* I said. *I know,* says the other bloke. *He's my mate and if you'd had as many trips as he has, you'd think you were a fucking car too. How many's he had?* I asked. *Thirteen,* came the answer. *We dipped a sheet of blotting paper in some liquid acid and we've been tearing strips off it all night.* I couldn't believe it! He went on: *I've had seven myself, dropped the lot on the way here. I was driving and it looked like there were people surfing on top of all the cars! Mate, you should've been there!* he says.

But the really funny thing is I saw the mad fucker again, a couple of months later, at a petrol station. I was talking to this girl and I saw him in her car. *Your mate's mad,* I said. *He thinks he's a car. You don't know the half of it,* she says. *Last week we found him lying in a puddle on his back telling people he was a swimming pool!*
Anon, London

I remember once I was in Ireland DJing and this little boy – he looked about ten – he came up to me in the middle of my set with what looked like a scrumpled up old flyer, and in the middle of it was a little pile of white powder. His little hand came up out of the crowd and offered it up to me and I looked down at this little face, looking ever so keen for me to partake of this white powder and so I said, *What's that?* And this little voice shouted up to me, *It's speed! It's speed!* He was very persistent so in the end I said, *Oh, go on then*, just to be sociable.

Another strange thing happened when I was DJing at Substation Soho and someone had a bit of a turn and jumped out of the crowd, straight through the hatch into the DJ booth, landing on top of both decks and the mixer, and just lay there. She did it all in one motion, very graceful. I don't know how she aimed herself through the hatch; it was quite miraculous. I think she was just after attention. She bent the arm of the needle, so I only had one deck to go on with. She didn't damage the other one, though, which was quite surprising. She tried hard enough.

Princess Julia, DJ, London

I went to Famous Five at Bagleys just after Christmas 1997. My sister bought me the ticket; she's a regular at Love Muscle at The Fridge and I'd gone there for a change a few weeks previously and loved it. I'm not gay, but I thought the atmosphere was brilliant and I still find that when I go to gay clubs now. There is a lot of really positive energy out there and you meet some really friendly people, apart from the fact that it makes a welcome change not to be leched at at every turn. That's not to say you don't get attention from gay guys at all – you do, especially if you're up there on a podium all night just flying – but it's positive, energising, affirmatory attention, instead of the demanding and predatory attention I'm more used to.

Anyway, when I went to Famous Five I wasn't really expecting to have a good time. I had a heavy cold and I felt like shite, and I'd only met most of the people we were going with that night. But I thought, what the hell, I'll give it my best shot.

We hadn't been there long and I was still waiting to come up on my speed. I was in the main room and the music was really going off, so I decided to get up on the stage. There weren't very many other people up there but it was a real focus for the rest of the room, which was rammed. There was another guy up there who was also really going for it, and he and I started dancing with each other, getting a real buzz off each other and off the crowd. Suddenly, he picked me up, turned me upside down and spun me round and round his head! As you can imagine, that brought me right up in the most massive rush, but that wasn't all; it turned out he's some kind of acrobatic performer, and he started lifting me up, twisting me around, throwing and spinning me on the stage in front of the crowd. It was amazing – I was flying from then on! It put me on a top buzz for the rest of the night.

I ended up having one of the best nights out I've ever had and met some wonderful people who were on a really good vibe and who gave out lots of positive energy. I hope that from my podium

I gave back to the crowd some of the energy I received from them and I feel privileged to have been part of such a brilliant crowd. It's one night I'll never forget.

Anon

the good times

It must have been to do with the time. My memories of it are tinged with an excited energy. A year in Brighton with Tom, Karen, Si, Viv, Jim and Ben. I'll never recreate the feeling. There wasn't an event as such, just mad weekends at the Zap. I thought we'd found the meaning of life.

I will never forget the nights we spent clubbing. It would start with blind panic as someone or other sped around town trying to sort out drugs, usually Karen or Tom. The house would buzz with the hectic schedule – getting ready, ringing everyone, arranging which bar to meet in, trips to the cashpoint and stuffing bags of pills down our shoes and Wonderbras. Then a short blur later, nervousness in the queue – would we get in? Would we survive the search on the door? Watching people pile into the club, feeling the atmosphere build. It's a time I find hard to describe, especially to people who were never there. It felt like we were part of a huge loved-up family. We were so young and naïve. There was no question that what we were doing was bad, everything revolved around getting to that point in the night when you'd given your whole body over to the music, the smiling faces, and the hugging. No matter how long I'd spent in anticipation of it, the feeling just came up behind me and swept me away – every time. I will never forget standing on one side of the dancefloor, looking around desperately for my friends, just wanting to find them and grab them and hold them. Usually I'd find two or three of them in a corner of the club just hanging on to each other, stroking each other's faces or massaging their shoulders. The bond was deeper than platonic, sexy in a pure way and something like the feeling between brothers and sisters.

I do not care how cheesy it sounds now because I will never write off the memory. If I could go back now, I would.

Daisey Bailey, Glasgow

When you take an E all else is shoved sideways. In the tumult of bodies and faces that assemble in clubs, you are but another punter gearing up for the plunge, ready for that moment when pill is pushed to mouth and gobbled down the great avenue of gleeful possibilities, the throat. Everything blurs. The music becomes a cathedral of sound, overwhelming, like a thousand operatic choirs raising you up to the maniac's platform where you trot and grin, inside and out, like an army of helium-crazed jokers . . .

Somehow I'd got the money together, as we all had, and into the car we jumped, shot through with magic at the prospect of the night ahead, and made our way down to the club. From Lancaster we arrived at the spot in around forty minutes, as I recall, and parked up outside. It was freezing, the lines of cars spilling out all the faithful denizens decorated in a variety of woolly hats, scarves, gloves, Timberland boots and puffa jackets, casting these members of the throng as chilblained Michelin men unaffected by the biting air. By the time it's our turn to be searched, I've already had a furtive feel of the pills and speed wraps nappy-pinned down my boxers and am confident that the security won't feel them. They're more concerned in posing and strutting in front of all the women in the queue, and as we enter, paying the money at the till, I cast a glance at the mirrored walls, having a quick ponder as to my chance of a pull tonight; I always fancy it, but once the E takes hold, then funny things happen, the kind of things that only dreams can parallel and cast as normal.

This is the ritual in its truest form. We are assembled at the same side as always, looking over on to the dancefloor, and begin to break the night in, lighting cigarettes, some of us buying beer, others sitting, while I pace around just in front of them, eyeing everyone and everything up. I am the rep for our group, the face of the crew. While they convene with each other, I'm more interested in all around me. I feel the vitality of the night like an alcoholic must crave his brew. I savour it all. It can't give me enough, this buzz, this gathering of crews, all of us alike yet different, the music beginning to really oil my senses, each new tune sliding into the night starting to build up, like the first few loving strokes of a perfect masturbation. Well, no, this is not quite fair, because although the night is primarily for me, although everyone is getting his rocks off for themselves, it is a celebration of life. When looking around, you see yourself reflected everywhere, not just in clothing and haircuts, but by the very presence of the people in the club, it is a wedding of attitude, the knowing grin that laughs at all the pen-pushers and their ilk.

I am standing by the railing and smoking a cigarette, when a lad I know walks up and shakes my hand. *All right, Willy,* I say, genuinely glad to see him. He has blond ringlets and a puffy face that could be described as angelic. It's funny how perceptions change as you get older. In the status league which keeps us all going, I'd always rated Willy as a non-starter, the kind of lad you see round town but never *out* of town on the higher stage. Now though, since first seeing him, both of us E'd up, in some club in Blackpool or Preston, I'd reconsidered, and am now easily engaged in the mutual appreciation which keeps all the world spinning round.

All right, Jake. How's it going?

All right Willy. I can't help casting my mind back though, to Monday, when me and Beano were trying to get hold of him for a score of Es. There was no reply and desperate for them as usual, we decided to have a drive up to his house, thinking that maybe he was out scoring at the time and would be back soon. Such are the desperate straws clutched at where drugs are involved. We got up there to find the house deserted, and so tried the back door, just in case. Willy lives out in the country, on a lane somewhere, and looking over his hedge, the fields seemed mournful and lonely as they dipped away from us over the horizon.

We knocked on the back door for a while, but having no luck, turned and were then presented with the clothes line and the prospect of a couple of tasty-looking items. However, not being born criminals, me and Beano shook our heads and walked back to the car. We were both keen but didn't have the bottle. *What d'you reckon?* Beano asked me, while we took a look up and down the lane. *Fuck it. You keep watch and I'll get 'em,* I said, turning towards the house, before stopping and shouting back to him in a muted whisper, *Get the motor running!* I swivelled and ran down the side of the house and into the back garden, grabbing the clothes off the line, shitting myself, yet completely delirious with laughter at what nice people we were; and then, reaching the car, I jumped into the front seat and we were away, me unable to stop laughing at the notion of us, the two most unlikely crooks in town, and all the time loving it more because it was such a dodgy trick ... You just don't seem to have any fun if you're a nice person. *Serves him right for not scoring us them Es*, I laughed. *Yeah, if he wasn't so full of shit then we wouldn't have done it.* Beano grinned, eyes gleaming.

And so here's Willy now. Park Hall nightclub, Thursday evening. Me trying not to laugh as he apologises for not scoring the pills for us. *Yeah, sorry about that*, he says. *I just couldn't get them anywhere.* The night was taking off all right. *Oh, it doesn't matter*, I assured him. *Have you got a cigarette by any chance?* He pulled it out and gave me it. *That same day, when you were supposed to come round, I had some clothes nicked off the washing-line.* He looked at me, disgusted. *You're joking aren't you? What was nicked?* I said, finding a well of sympathy I myself was surprised at. *A pair of jeans and a jumper*, he said, naming the brand. *Fucking hell, that's a shitty trick*, I said. *They're nice jeans those as well. I've got a pair. Look, I've got 'em on now.* I pulled my jacket up and showed him the jeans. After this encounter I wander back over to my lot, chuckling to myself and relate the whole thing to Beano, who can only laugh and wonder whether he should've worn the jumper as well.

By now it's time to take the E, so we sit there looking out into the half-light, people passing by on their way to whichever spot is the one for them. Tonight it's brown biscuits and we discuss their smacky reputation, how we could be gouched out for the evening, pinned against the wall, grinning through jammed-down eyelids, concentrating on the music as it smoothly courses through us like fuel propelled at a hundred miles an hour. This is what we hope for. I've never had a dud yet. And so I stand, and attached to the music's umbilical, am pulled towards the railing in a half-trance. It all washes over me, up me, through me, the piano becoming a war chant telling me now is the time, *now is the time.*

When I put the tablet in, I have to crunch it, since I can't swallow anything whole, and the bitter taste rips over my tongue and down my throat, and gasping I grab someone's water and wash it down, retching yet wanting it, straight away. I reckon I can feel it coming up; but no, it'll be twenty minutes before anything actually does take grip, causing my arse to cave and a sudden need to race to the toilet; this, of course, being the regular routine whenever anything exciting's on the cards.

This is fifteen minutes in and so I stagger to the upstairs toilet, through the mass of punters who are now starting to transform the club into an upraised Hades; Hades being the operative word as any biblical heaven could never equal this drug plus club that dizzies my senses, like I'm teetering on a screaming gorge's edge, whilst dancing to the tune of the little fairies that skip inside of me like skewered nymphs. I am not all out for drugs. I reckon like anything else you can have too much, but I know for sure that if nothing else, everyone should have at least one E, because that one pill, the first, is like nothing you've ever had. A course of acid, speed and dope can't prepare you for it. It's like expecting to walk only realising you can fly, and you're not only flying, you're singing, gloriously, about an assault on the senses, the closest comparison being some gorgeous piece of music that caves the earth away, leaving you totally infatuated with everything around you. And that's why people go back after the first one, for another go, and then another, trying to catch that buzz; but after the first month or two on them, things start to change, and slowly the gear, the music, the whole scene, starts to get at you. Imperceptibly at first, but before long it *does* begin to bite.

By this time, I'd reached the toilets, and in I went, through the familiar door and waited my turn for the cubicle, standing there feeling goofier and goofier by the second. It was five minutes before I noticed it was out of order, and all the time the shit was pressing. Beginning to panic a bit, I half-trotted across the crowded floor, grimacing when I thought no one was looking and forcing a smile when I thought they were, before finally I reached the toilet on the far side and bundled myself in, locking the door behind me. I tore my jeans and boxers down and gratefully touched my arse to the cold china when BANG!!! the lights went out, accompanying the delivery of my first log. The release of that bundle of fun together with the complete darkness brought the E right up, and I sat there pissing myself laughing, feeling all the hairs on me standing up as I began to rush. Then it was time to find the toilet paper, and not being familiar with its exact strategic position, I struggled, fumbling along the wall, before I finally found it. I now stood up, trying not to fall over under the force of the E, which was like a great hand yanking me to and fro by the hair as I wiped my backside, while all I could do was giggle at myself, crouched over, trying not to miss too many bits. And of course, this all set me up for a good night. I mean, how could I fail after this? I walked out of there to find the rest like a drunken sailor.

This allusion to being drunk may seem strange, whether you've done Es or not, but this part of them, when they first come up and your legs fold, you find it hard to speak, and everything seems slurred, off kilter, is just like being pissed. Of course it's all subjective, as different people are affected differently, as with other drugs. I mean, I've got friends who never ever have bad trips; c'mon now . . .

It was nearing the end of the night when after a second E, and feeling completely goosed, I found myself at the railings, looking down on to the dancefloor, even shaking some moves myself, when up walked what later became known as 'The Whale'. At the time she was gorgeous, just what I needed, feeling like that: a big pair of luscious female lips. We locked horns like wildebeests, electricity coursing through my teeth, and when I broke for air, Beano and his lady friend, Tessa, were having a good old laugh whilst looking amazed at how quickly the deal had been struck. They weren't the only ones. Before I knew it, I was saying goodbye to all of them and was on my way in a car to her place somewhere near Chorley.

At her house there were a few gathered, as there inevitably are after a night out on the Es. I settled down in the lounge on the sofa, smoking dope and chatting to whoever walked in and out from the kitchen. 'The Whale', I forget her name, wandered to and fro at intervals, making sure I was okay and not going to come to my senses before the big one, while I began to notice the group of lads sitting round the telly on the other side of the room. There was a scouser, and some others from Preston. They pulled some trips out and ate them, offering me one, which I refused, not wanting to spoil a good night and we all began chatting about God knows what. Through the frosted kitchen door, I saw a group of lads walk in and sit down at the table. One of them was a lad I knew, named Quaz, who was the local E dealer. Seeing my chance, I pulled 'The Whale' the next time she walked in and sat her down on the sofa.

Lend us fifteen quid for an E? I pleaded, suddenly excited at the thought of another pill and all it would mean, but she was reluctant, not trusting me for some reason. *I don't know* she said. *I lent this lad some money last week and he still hasn't given me it.* Ignoring the implications of that comment, I pressed on, saying, *Look, lend me the fifteen, and tomorrow I'll pay his debt and mine back. How?* she asked. *If you give us a lift back then I'll run in and get it.* I was desperate now, but I knew I had her. After all, I was her guest, and if she wanted to secure the shag then there was nothing else for it.

She walked to the kitchen and got a couple of doves from Quaz and brought them back, giving me one. I shoved it down my mouth, crunching away as usual and prepared myself for the onslaught. Meanwhile, over in the corner, Mickey the scouser and his cronies took out another trip and downed it. The night was beginning to warm up. 'The Whale' disappeared upstairs and I settled back into conversation again with them, keeping an eye on the kitchen scene through the frost. Part of me was wishing I was in there, sitting round the table with the boys, having a power chat about the evening's E sales, dishing them out to my mates and laughing and smoking with the good secure feel of a wad of money in my pocket, like no doubt Quaz and the rest of them had. He owned a bleeper, even then, in 1991, which for the north of England had to mean he was smart and upwardly mobile. At this time, just becoming aware of the scene and the dealers, I felt an aura whenever I saw the smart boys in their designer jackets and crews, drinks in one hand, the next sale of pills in the other, having a laugh and a joke, everyone's friend.

Now, I see through all that, knowing that a lot of these characters got caught and sent down. I might think I'm tough in some ways, but being able to handle prison isn't one of them. Yet at the same time it is a fair old life, selling pills and being free, if you can pull it off, and those who do deserve all they get. Some may say they're supplying potential death, others that they are crooks and thugs, and I'd agree that this is true, but then no one forces drugs down people's throats and there's far more crooks in the government, sending people to die in wars, and not paying for proper hospital care. The world's a hypocritical place. I'm a hypocrite, you're a hypocrite. Stand up, be proud of it. Like anything with an ounce of danger and excitement, there'll always be pitfalls, but with danger comes gain, a sense of exhilaration, and that's what I was feeling sitting there listening to scouse Mickey crack jokes to us, the plebs, while the monarchy sat in a normal suburban kitchen and turned it into a modern-day amphitheatre for my eyes.

By this time, five or six in the morning, the boys were due another trip. In fact, a blond-haired lad pulled the whole sheet out and counted what was left. *Sixteen*, he said, *c'mon, let's do 'em all, that's four each.* This got me all right. By now I was sat on a chair directly behind them, resting against the back wall of the room. They turned and offered me one, but I refused, pissing myself at the whole situation. Es make you feel silly anyway, but for fuck's sake, watching four lads do six trips each over a couple of hours, when one would have me climbing the walls for my mother, just rounded it all off: it was a classic, to be remembered and treasured like a great music tape.

By seven in the morning we were all bosom friends. Some of the banter that had kicked around was ridiculous. I mean, I'd been at school only a couple of years earlier and now I was sat in some girl's front room near Preston, watching breakfast telly with a bunch of trip-heads, on a sofa which was feeling like laughter under my legs. My body was fizzing, my head buzzed, I had a joint on the go, and I was letting the soft, luscious house music fill me from the corner, where the fire glowed a sliver of life right through all our youth.

At seven thirty, Mickey got up from the chair he'd sat in all night and pulled his coat on, saying, *Right, that's me lads, got to get back for work in Liverpool for nine. Where d'you work?* I asked. *On the buses mate* he replied. *On the number 45 route, driving loads of screaming school kids.* He felt round in his pockets, then looked at us, eyes like saucers. *No trips left by any chance?* We shook our heads in regret, then had a fumble around on the floor just in case, but there was no saving him. I felt like asking him why he needed more, but I knew it wouldn't register.

All right then, see ya. Saying this, he walked over to me, grabbed my face and planted a big sloppy kiss on my forehead. I was a little surprised. *Are you at Park Hall next week?* he asked. *Certainly will be, wouldn't miss it* I replied.

He stood swaying in the room considering its topness, while the bloke on the breakfast telly announced it was going to be a cold day. *Right then see ya all.* He took one last look at the room and us through his mop of curls and left.

I looked at the clock on the telly. It said eight-fifteen. Mickey had taken an hour to say goodbye. It had to be time to face 'The Whale'.

See you in a bit then lads. I felt almost embarrassed. What had been a good score last night, one for the crack, the laugh, was now being shown for what it was: a cold whimper of a shag. I didn't know what was worse: the fact that I didn't fancy her, or that, even if I *had* got it in, I would've come within ten seconds. I mean, two pills, no sleep and copious amounts of dope could mean only one thing: a quick thrash, come like gangbusters, and then *zzzzzzzzzzzzzzzzzzzzzzzz* off to sleep. She probably wasn't missing too much anyway. Cunnilingus with my mouth would have been like kissing her down there with forty-year-old sandpaper . . .

Up the stairs I went, sliding my hand along the wooden bannister before walking into the room, hoping she was asleep. She wasn't. Getting in, I began to warm to the idea. It was all right under here with the duvet wrapped round me all smooth like her jelly legs never could. I got a hard-on. The blood rose. JESUS!!! This was fucking great. I wanted to shag the quilt, it was getting to me where it hurt. 'The Whale' placed her hand on my dick and then that was that. I mean, she was a nice enough lass, but her hand was cold and my dick was hot; talk about a clash. Down it drooped like a sad old man. But still the E did its stuff, refusing to give up. I stared up at the ceiling and watched as slowly its whiteness broke waves across my legs, bringing the buzz right back. I mumbled something to her, and then turned over, feeling my hard-on rage up again. Slowly but surely I began to wank.

Until . . .

Yes . . .

Oh yes . . .

The duvet got it.

True love.

Just like in the movies.

Around three in the afternoon I slowly came around from a recurring dream I'd been having. It consisted of me being desperate for a piss, taking a piss, only to need another a minute later. In came Orca with a cup of tea.
Jamie Jackson, London

So warm inside, I've just swallowed the sun
So far beyond, another week's won.
A blast, a horn, that sweet bass sound;
Blows me away every time.
The beautiful people . . . That sweet bass sound
Swirling around like a cork on the sea.
The sound of the music sets you free.
Everybody loves my shirt, all the girls seem to flirt.
I'm just so far beyond,
Laughing at a tinkle, a bleep, a wobble, and that sweet bass sound.
Then it's just distance, riding the wave.
Swimming, your mind's swimming.
Then the thoughts, regrets or triumphs.

Then alone, deep away inside.

Alone.

Or not.

And all those beautiful people are strangers.

I hope I don't see them again, not now.

Next week maybe, but please not now.

The bus ride home – everyone knows how it is.

The police siren in the fresh, crisp morning. It couldn't be that
bad . . .

I dream of my bed. Head down. I dream of dreaming.

Sweet smoke, idle talk, giggles, a warm drink . . .

Or warming.

I see myself so far below.

All warm, never alone.

And I see those beautiful people again.

And they bring that sweet bass sound,

It blows me away every time.

And again I join the land of the happy.

Anton Garby, Brixton

A remember the old days before drugs became the norm, no that
a've anything against them, in fact a would actively encourage
them. Ye see a grew up in the days when gaun oot for a bevy was
the thing to do, occasionally havin' the odd line a speed. Mind
you, ye only took that so ye could bevvy that bit longer. Sayin'
that though, there was the older crew that were daein' blackies,
chalkies and blues when the northern soul scene was big, but that
seemed to be a phase and didnae really last that long.

Drink hus never really been a good drug fur me or fur maist people come tae think ae it. Aw that shite you hud to put up wae. Ye could be standin' in a boozer wi' yer mates and some cunt would just catch your eyes then it would be:

Who you looking at pal, goat a problem?

Me, mate? Na nowt wrong wi' me.

Think yer a wide cunt dae ye?

There was no way ye could talk yer way oot, because ye knew he was blootered. Then one ae yer mates would ask if there was a problem and all hell would break loose and if ye were lucky naebody goat a tumbler in the face.

The other side tae it was the sheer embarrassment that bevy can cause oan a night oot, and ye see it comin'. One minute ye appear tae be stone cold sober, then the next yer making a complete cunt ae yersel'. It was generally the phone call the next mornin' fae one ae yer mates that cut deep.

Mornin', you just oot yer scratcher? What a night and what about you boy, ya fuckin' doughnut. Ye wait a few seconds then decide ye huv tae know what happened last night.

Aye, what the fuck happened then? A cannae remember.

You know that wee bird Jane, well ye were tryin' tae put the bite on her, and she just wusnae huvin' it, so she eventually, eftir you pesterin' her fur aboot an oor, she told ye were a fuckin' arsehole in front ae every cunt and would ye mind fuckin' off somewhere tae die.

This type ae thing was a killer especially as ye thought she might have fancied ye. Ye hud no choice though, ye either pulled that night or ye were classed as some kind ae poofter. The pressure was intense and ye hud tae score wi' a bird. Except a fair bit ae the time ye made a tit ae yersel'. The only option left was tae go oot the next night and make an even bigger cunt ae yersel' than ye did the night before, the big spiral ae drink.

A remember the first night a dropped an E. It was up in Edinburgh in a boozer called the Moscow bar. A mate said they had been daein' it for aboot a year and it was a different class. A went intae a big lecture aboot Russian roulette and shite like that but eftir a fair while a was tempted enough tae try a half. It was a wee dove when they were still sound. That night a knew a would fight it, which was exactly what a done. A never really goat that much fae it, maybe a mild sense of well-being. A went hame that night tae ma ma's hoose and intae ma old bed a hud as a kid. When a woke up the next day eftir a bit ae a worrying night's sleep, a felt as if ma kidneys were in agony and a was convinced that acute renal failure was settin' in. As a worked oot later, this was aw in the mind, i.e. am still alive and well.

So that first wee dabble intae E was nowt tae shout home aboot, nondescript really. The next time was also back up in Edinburgh and a was in a much more 'up for it' mood as they say in the scene these days. A was oot wi' a good crowd and felt in a good mood. Everybody popped one in the City Café then we aw shot doon the road tae Yip Yap at La Belle Angele. It took about half an hour tae kick in, but a just remember standing aroond the dance area and whoosh, fuck what a rush, a was right ontae the dancefloor. A wee lad ma brar knew, cannae remember ayes name, knew he was an apprentice ae some sort oan the buildin' sites, we just danced aw night in a corner.

A think it crossed ma mind fleetingly, what the fuck huv a been daein' fur the last few years. Mind you a was too busy huvin the best night ae ma life tae gae too much thought tae anything. A've always luved dancin' like a loon, but that was looked on in the auld days as like, *who's that arse?* Now a can dance like fuck and not one person takes one bit ae notice 'cause they're aw too busy in thair ain happy wee worlds, and good on them.

The only downer fae that night was it finished aroond aboot three or four and a could huv danced aw night. We aw went back tae ma brar's and listened tae some mair sounds, then a went and crashed oot. When a woke the next day a felt fine, nain ae the bullshit ye read aboot in the paper.

It was the next day that a thought aboot what a hud moved intae and a knew in ma heart that this was gonnae change ma life fur the better. Lookin' back on it now two years later, it hus. A love the pumpin' sounds ae progressive house and techno. Ye cannae but no dance tae that music. When a go tae a club a normally never get any bother. The worst that can happen tae ye is tae git hugged tae death. A understand that a lot ae the mates that ye make are just fur that night, it's the drugs and that. Who gives a fuck so long as ye have a good night and ye dinnae git yer face punched in. There is still a few bevy merchant arseholes but they're in the minority now.

In the past a used tae suffer fae depression. It was a continuing struggle, but now a go oot tae various clubs, drop an E and aw ma worries melt away. Yeah, it's temporary, but overall ma attitude tae life is much more positive than it ever hus been. The medical profession can recommend Prozac. Well a would prescribe a good Dove or even better a Robin and a Laidman stompin' compilation and come back and tell ayes life's no that much better.

The only regret ave goat is that am no twenty again 'cause what the younger generation huv goat is much better than ma ain formative years. Ave been lucky though, even the fact that a came tae this scene much later than maist, it's been good, really good. Am now thirty-three, in a professional joab and a might in the future seem like a bit ae a sad cunt if a was in a club dancin' aboot, so aye know a might only huv anar few years ae this left, but am gaun tae enjoy every fuckin' minute as a huv done in the past.

A hope the younger generation comin' through keep at it, whatever shape it evolves intae because no matter what wankers in suits think, it's no gonnae go away, well no yet anyway.

In a few years' time a might well be oan the golf 'cause a do enjoy a game ae golf. A might even drop one oan the course, might huv the best round ae golf in ma life, par the bastard. Ah'll look back and think a special wee dove ae peace brought me ma ain personal sort ae contentment, no bad fur an auld fart, eh?

Gary P, Newcastle

Biology, Watford, 10 June 1989: This was a 'private party', so we had to get membership cards done beforehand. The organisers had paid for the farmer who owned the site to go to Spain for the weekend so that the police couldn't hassle him or put pressure on him to change his mind. We'd been worried about the weather; it had been raining all week and we knew there was only one marquee there and that was strictly VIPs. Anyway, we got there at about midnight and it packed up late afternoon. The stage was the biggest I've seen to this day, with a massive scaffolding tower to one side; I remember seeing some bloke hanging off it at one point, totally off it. I met him later. *Do you remember that geezer hanging off the scaffold at Biology?* I asked. *Yeah mate, that was me!* he said. *I was tripping off my nut, mate, I was so fucking off it ...* Then, in the morning, the MC started giving us the weather forecast. It was surreal. Then he started saying, *STOP! STOP! EVERYONE JUST STOP!* and eventually they did, and the DJ stopped and we all looked at him. *Everyone turn around and look at that sun,* he says, and we did, and the sun was blazing in the sky and it was a beautiful day ...

Biology built its reputation on that event. It got amazing write-ups, and they never did another one that matched it.
Simon, London

I've been clubbing in and around London for a few years now, but it was only a couple of months ago that I discovered Kool Eddy's. You'd never know it was there unless someone took you, and that's the beauty of it. It may be in the heart of the West End, but it has to be London clubland's best-kept secret.

I'd been out all the night before to a club on Oxford Street which I'd never been to before, partly because I knew it was very small and partly because it mainly played house, and my clubbing roots are in techno. But I went because I had a friend to stay, and she wanted to go out, and I was broke and it was cheap. And despite my reservations I had a brilliant night out.

The club was definitely the friendliest I've ever been to. I made friends that night I still have now, and I make more every time I go. The mix of people was really diverse – gay and straight, black and white, scruffy and glammed-up: a real example of the tolerance, friendliness and sense of family that a good club can produce out of a room full of total strangers. The atmosphere was laid back; although there is the odd frisson of interest to spice up an evening, it's not a meat market, which is good. Most girls I know go out to dance, not to pull, and unwelcome attention is a drag. And although I now go there regularly, the only 'trouble' I've ever witnessed was from pissed-up beer monsters, not clubbers, and even they usually leave of their own accord when they see no one is interested and they aren't going to get a rise out of such a chilled crowd.

The word began to go around at about three am. *Coming down the caff after?* I heard. *Coming over the road?* What the hell, we thought; it was cheaper than getting a cab home. At least this way we could save money by waiting somewhere warm until the Tube started running.

When it was time for the club to kick out, you didn't have to ask directions. Everyone who had lasted the distance piled around the corner, over the road, and up the dingy narrow stairs. Now, Kool Eddy's (or 'the Caff') isn't much to look at, but it is much loved by its regular clientele and fiercely defended from 'riff raff', unwelcome elements, and those on the wrong vibe. But most importantly of all there is a DJ, and the 'dancefloor' is usually full of those (like me) who just can't get enough, who just can't sit still whilst there's a tune playing. And there are 'characters', who come every week from God only knows where, and the occasional dog or tramp.

So there the party continues for a few more hours – precious time for the conversations you can't have when the music is deafening, for the cup of tea you've been gasping for, and for phone numbers to be exchanged and assignations made. It's a bridge from the previous night into the cold light of day, helping to let you down gently into the harsh, real world and the seemingly endless week to come.

Mel, London

In the queue
God it's cold.
There's nothing to do but wait.
I wait in anticipation of the next few hours.
Those hours will seem like minutes,
I'll be walking in one minute
and the next it'll be over and
I'll be shaking hands and talking to those around me.

I'm waiting in the queue
I can hear the music through the wall
it's loud and I can't wait to get in there.

Ahead of me people snake around
the corner of the building.
Everyone is cold, especially the girls,
some of them are wearing next to nothing,
later on they'll be fucking hot, sweating.
I chose not to wear a jumper as
I don't fancy waiting in the queue
for half an hour at the end of the night,
instead I queue in a T-shirt and necklace.

The cloakroom ticket would be one more thing
to think and worry about.
Money, fags, keys, wallet, stash –
in my undies.
Can't have the security finding that.

I can feel my first half starting to work.
It's so obvious that those around me can
also feel theirs as some stranger
grabs my hand and asks,
Awright, where you from bud?
The Lake District, I reply.
I've long since given up saying *Barrow in Furness* or *Cumbria,*
as nobody knows where the fuck that is, even though it is only
an hour and a half up the M6.
The stranger carries on:
Oh yeah, what you having tonight then?
Now I'm always wary when I'm asked this question because no
matter what you've had they've always had more.
But for now, coming up, my inhibitions are removed and I
reply,
A couple of Doves and a wrap.
Oh yeah, I've just downed one and I'm fucked already.
I smile and say,
Nice one.
What's your name, bud?
Mike. What's yours?
Dave.
Nice to meet you Dave, I say
and we shake hands again.
Been here before?
Yeah, once or twice.
The queue moves on and we step forward.
I catch my mate's eye standing behind me and he makes a
funny face.

Dave seems to have run out of things to say,
Fucking cold innit? he says in a desperate attempt to keep the
conversation alive.
Yeah, too fucking right, I reply and we both look away.
The conversation is dead
but I have to admire this
whole situation.
Dave would never have shaken my hand and spoken to me
if he had been drinking beer.
This situation provides an excellent
argument for the legalisation of drugs.
Two complete strangers shaking hands
and talking with trust like the best
of friends.
No one gets aggressive, no one starts fights,
everyone's there to dance and have a good time
together.

I approach the front door
and empty my pockets as the
steroid-pumped guard searches my pockets.
I see Dave, just ahead, going in,
See ya later, he shouts back.
I nod at him and smile.
Michael N. Gibbs, Stoke-on-Trent

Euphoria – it's the only way I can describe it. You're in a club
and you've taken a gram or three of speed. It doesn't hit you

straight away but the anticipation is almost as good as the experience itself. Fellow clubbers are giving it loads on the dancefloor and you know it's only a matter of time before you're out there with them.

Then it hits you – the tingle factor! It's as though you have pins and needles EVERYWHERE, as though a can of something incredibly fizzy has been shaken up and opened inside you. And then the transformation takes place. You become the best dancer in the club, in the country, in the whole world! At least, that's the way it feels! Nothing can stop you – literally. You have so much energy you just have to move. It's like an amazing rush that has to be released and the only way you can do it is to dance.

There are people moving on fast-forward everywhere and you are one of them. It's such a unifying experience. You may have lost sight of your friends hours ago but it doesn't matter. Everybody is experiencing the same sense of euphoria. Everyone is smiling, happy, and everyone wants to dance. Nothing else matters. Once you enter a club and you experience that unmistakable feeling, dancing is your top priority.

Six or seven hours later the club closes. We are all thrown back into the real world and our priorities change, but only until next weekend.

Karen, Liverpool

It was the same story, Friday evening and someone pipes up, *Free party in Wales tomorrow. Anyone coming?*

Saturday night came and we set off for Wales. After stopping for certain lightweights to spew up, we finally got to the venue. Eh up, no fuckin' party. Just a Land-Rover and a few pissed-off ravers.

The geezer in the Landy said, *Follow me to another party*, so off we went. Ten miles later a convoy of us arrived in a small lane. Some dodgy-looking bloke asked for a fiver a head to get in. So, five quid later we were told to follow the lane and that it was a long way. Coming up on the speed, I started to think this is a wind-up (by the time we realise there is no party, the Landy and the dodgy geezer would be gone), but we carried on. Eventually we stopped, almost certain we had been done out of a fiver, but as soon as we turned the engine off, we heard a rockin' 'B'-line. At that instant the speed kicked it. I was up. We followed the lane some more until we reached hundreds of cars parked either side of the lane. We found the party and it was fuckin' boomin', two systems, food tent, lost property tent, mountains of speakers. But the two most important points were loads of twisted people and no Old Bill.

The night progressed, getting better all the time, and then the sun rose. What a sun, what heat. Everything was bang on.

All this led to our crew doing our own free parties. We've only done two and they weren't too bad. Inevitably the Old Bill turned up, but they were sound as a pound, letting the first one carry on, and at the second one we were just putting the generator back in the van, but again no attitude from them.

Why can't it always be like this?
Jim Gregory (Coventry Kru), Coventry

I met Tanya on New Year's Eve 1994. If you want me to be precise it was around three am on 1 January 1995 but you get the picture. On New Year's Eve itself we (me and my crazy flatmates) decided to go on a real bender to see the New Year in. I bought a long kilt (and I proceeded to have many enquiries to see if I was wearing any underwear beneath it). I guess I looked a bit of a gay icon because I had a tight white T-shirt and big boots on to compound the image.

That night I went to Fierce Child at Mars, which is next door to the Astoria on Tottenham Court Road. Fat Tony was playing and because we were in a big group we stood out from the rest of the crowd. I was in a pretty messy state when I saw her. She stood out in her own special way in a silver sequinned dress and long black hair. We moved closer and started talking loud and saying nothing. I'll always remember the next words she uttered. My friend really fancies you, she said. I turned round and saw a male friend of hers shuffling away. I said, That's nice but I'm not that way inclined, to which she replied, Well I'll take your number then. We were together after that night for a year and a half and have become very good friends, nattering about relationships, careers, etc., etc. She used to tell me about her wild nights out where she really pushed the edge, so when I told her about this book, she jumped at the chance of getting the details of a particularly mad night on the page . . .

Dalston was the place; December 1993 was the time. The party had the original title of Goa Party, which sets the scene for the weirdest party I've ever been to. The promoters were a bunch of rich, international party-goers who set up parties around the world. This particular soirée was based in a disused warehouse in east London on a sparkling full-moon night. This party wanted to recreate the music and atmosphere coming out of Goa.

My friend Riz had met the promoters in Goa and had kept in touch with them because she enjoyed caning it with them so much. The other people who came with us that night were Bernie, Sam, Simon the Halo, Cowboy, Steve Stone and his girlfriend who looked like a rough pikey from Feltham. They picked me up from my house in Brentford and we began the long journey across town to the party.

We were glad the party was on because around this time the police were pretty clued up about illegal do's and raids on parties were commonplace. The warehouse was decked out in fluorescent blue light with pink and yellow harps and globes hanging from the roof and orange branches around the side. The floor was carpeted and this would take on greater significance later in the night. People got straight on with the business of sorting themselves out with drugs (more than most forms of music, drugs are needed to really appreciate trance at its best). We got some blue microdots, which a lot of people will remember because they were so strong! I had a dance first but Simon necked a full one straight away. We also got our hands on some Es and we had a run-in with some acid punch, which brought me up so fast I almost hit the roof.

The music that was spinning was sixties' psychedelia rather than trance at first and the carpet started rising and shimmering with the music. The combination of pills and punch made it really hard work trying to ride the music, but you had to, otherwise you could lose it so badly you would either start screaming or go into regression. The effect was like being hypnotised (dictionary definition: a trance-like condition in which the subject is in a state of altered consciousness).

Maybe it was the fact that we had different stuff from Simon or maybe it was because he did a whole microdot at once, but he lost it. Big Time. I was really enjoying the hallucinations (dictionary definition: the apparent perception of sights, sounds, etc. that are not actually present). Before I'd left the house that night I had read about Adam and Eve in the Bible. After Eve had talked to Satan who told them they were naked, Adam and Eve proceeded to cover themselves up. When God discovered them he said, *Who told you that you were naked?* This passage came back into my mind because my friends said to me without knowing I had read this, *He looks like Adam*, while pointing to Simon the Halo. He was standing in the middle of the rave with a fluorescent harp and bow and arrow he had picked up from the ceiling. Also he was completely butt naked! He had removed his clothes at some point during the evening and now looked like Cupid with an oversized bow. I honestly thought it was the visuals, but my friends went up and talked to him, and I realised it was for real. The sight of Bernie and Riz talking to a naked man had me in stitches. I told Simon's mate about him, but he said *fuck him*, so Sam, Bernie, Riz and I had to try and help him out.

We started talking to him, calling his name, but he couldn't remember who he was. In fact, all he did was start talking like a baby. While all this was happening I kept hearing water and it reinforced the image of him as a Greek god. Sam went to the promoters because she was worried at this point. They tried to chill her out by saying that she should let him get on with it and enjoy the experience. But they didn't have to explain to his parents the next day. People were gawping at poor Simon so we decided to get him out of the rave and into the van. We put him in the back and got into the front seats. The van could not be moved because cars were parked all around it, so all we could do was look at a brick wall, which freaked us out less than Simon, who we couldn't bear to look at.

When we got back to Feltham we were so fucked we didn't want any of the neighbours seeing what we looked like, so we backed the van right up to the front door. Simon sobered up later on and we asked him if he remembered what had happened. He said the rave hadn't been a rave for him. He'd played on a Sega Megadrive before he had gone out and he'd thought he was still inside that machine, and that everyone he touched sparked. Simon definitely changed after that night out. A couple of weeks later he started going to Trade with a Barbie doll tied around his neck, which was quite strange for someone who was such a lad.

It took us a couple of days to come down from that night. People go out all the time trying to get the best buzz ever and we reached that point that night. I've never been able to achieve that level since. It's probably because the microdots and pills we had were pure, whereas these days they are cut with all sorts of crap just to make you buy more in the vain attempt to get 'really high'. When you're on acid it is both a mental and spiritual journey and we'd reached the crossroads at that party. You can either hold on to yourself, or you can go beyond that point, but then what sort of person would you become? I think Simon went beyond 'that point'. He went through a rebirth that night. The party made you feel like you were being hypnotised; it could have been me who stripped off but I didn't, which I am very glad about. One thing's for sure, tranceheads know how to party. They're people ahead of their time in music, dance and dress.

Tanya Quarrie *interviewed by* **Colin Peters, London**

It was June 1995 and we'd been driving along the border for about an hour and a half and we were starting to get a bit pissed off. We wouldn't have cared if we'd been in the middle of the Far East, but we weren't. We were crawling along the edge of Northamptonshire.

We hoped the party was just around every bend we reached, but I suppose we were just all being optimistic because we were sure we must have passed it. But then, there it was, scrawled on a piece of cardboard in letters about half a foot high: STRAWBERRY PICKERS. We knew it was next left, which turned out to be what looked like an access track.

We soon met a line of stationary cars, and still couldn't see the site, but we knew we were there. We couldn't be bothered to drive any further, so we jumped out of the car and walked down the track. People were sitting in their cars, windows down, skinning up and edging forward a few feet every minute or so.

Then somebody came running out of the trees in front of us shouting, *You can get in down here!* At this, all of the cars within hearing distance emptied, and about twenty people plus at least as many again from other cars close by who had cottoned on were running through the trees, over a fence and up a hill. It could only have been a few hundred yards, but then we heard the bass. It must have been well sound-proofed because it was in this bowl of a valley with trees all up the sides.

Once we hit the top of the hill we could see the party down below us: no tents, just a tower with the sound system and lights on, and platforms around it which were covered in speakers and brightly coloured decorations. Someone said the sound system was Skylab, which made sense as they'd been doing a fair few parties that year.

There looked to be about five hundred or so people there already, although we only had the lights to go by. There would be thousands more by the next day. *Fucking yes!* somebody shouted and everybody was laughing as we ran down the other side of the hill, dodging the trees, towards the party.

We could see now why the cars had been so slow-moving. At the 'official' site entrance there was a group of blokes trying to direct traffic into a tiny area set aside for them, but there wasn't enough room so people were driving anywhere they could. Towards the end of the night a girl we met told us it got worse later on, because further up the track people had abandoned their cars to avoid the 'door', and no other cars could get past! *That was us*, we told her; she'd had to park on the proper road quite a walk from the track, and apparently there were cars bumper to bumper all along the verges in both directions.

We'd been stockpiling our drugs for days, so we had loads to go between us. We'd already had some whizz so it was a good half-hour before we found a spot where we wanted to build a fire and take some more drugs, after walking around to see if we could see anyone else we knew.

An hour later and we had well and truly come up on our Es. The site looked magical: lights were bouncing off the trees, and the techno was just getting louder and louder. The valley was full of people and there were fires burning all around the massive crowd dancing and shouting around the sound system. I swear E has never been as good as it was on that night; we were all totally off it.

Then some people dancing on the speakers started pointing up into the sky behind us, and everybody turned around to see a helicopter coming towards us with its beam scanning the site. We hadn't been able to hear it coming above the music, but we could feel it now as the powerful searchlight fucked with our eyes. It was the police, who had to turn up some time. They flew off again and it was at least half an hour before they came back, this time in vanloads, crawling down the track as slowly as our cars had before them.

They got out of the vans and one of them came over flanked by a couple of others and remonstrated with some bloke who was sitting on the back bumper of one of the trucks the set-up had arrived in. As we all watched the altercation, the music was turned down and people started whistling.

But then the best thing happened. The inspector (or whoever it was) turned around and walked away, the music was pumped up again, and the police vans reversed back up the hill! It didn't take a genius to work out that once the party had kicked in, there would be more chaos in breaking it up than in letting it continue. No police force would want that many cars on their roads full of so many people who were fucked.

What could have ruined the night turned out to make it. The guy on the van who had argued with the police came jumping around shouting, *Free acid! Free acid!* And so it was; he had a bag crammed full of microdots and he was pressing them into people's hands. He must have had a fair few of them himself because no sane person would throw that much money down people's necks for free. I reckon at least a hundred people had a very confused night from that point on, thanks to him. I was certainly completely nutted.

All I can remember for the rest of the night was being off my face half-dancing, half-stumbling around, thinking I was dancing like a pro, although I can't have been because I seemed to spend most of my time lying down. I can't remember seeing my mates for hours but as I started getting it together dawn was breaking, and there were a hell of a lot more people there than I could remember. I ended up sitting in some bloke's car, who I had met while he was skinning up his gear, when some girl started running around screaming her head off and jumping on to the bonnets of cars. Nobody was bothered by this, though; everyone just acted like it was totally normal! Eventually she disappeared – fuck knows where – but we saw her later on, canny as fuck with a smile pasted across her face. Somebody had given her something nice, I thought.

We left in the middle of the afternoon the next day, all of us still off it, but we had to get back to London. Apparently it went on for days before the police finally broke it up. But we'd had our fun by then, and it was probably somewhere else the next weekend.

J, London

the bad times

the bad times

I don't want to start moralising about drugs, I love 'em too much, but I would like to tell you about the night I nearly died. Or at least that's what I thought was happening at the time.

It was a couple of years ago. The whole white-glove, Vicks-embalming ritual thing had died the death a long time before, or at least been budged out of the way by the swinging hips of glam clubbing. I never really was into the whole fashion aspect. God, when I first started 'drug' clubbing I was a hob-nail-boots-nose-ring-and-plaits girl. I just went along with my mates every week to witness a completely new world from a very different, chemically-induced state of head, and sort of got into it that way. Being a guitar girl at heart (which I still very much am) it wasn't even the music, it was the drugs and the atmosphere. Mind you, saying that, '91 and '92 were the years when a lot of dance music got ever so slightly dodgy anyway. I'd missed the explosion of the late eighties. Better late than never, eh? It was an amazing time none the less. The air had such a feeling of wild abandonment and pure hedonistic fun – at any cost. Anyway, I digress.

The Music Factory in Sheffield was putting on a Stateside weekender which was basically a whole host of trendy US DJs playing a two-night extravaganza. We'd been looking forward to this one for weeks and weeks, and a truck-load of our mates were coming up for it. We intended a substance-fuelled, sleep-deprived, whoop-holler of a weekend. Oh yes!

The Friday night was a complete ball. We'd originally said that we were going to try and take it easy – didn't want to be too fucked for the Saturday night. Mmm, that one didn't quite work out. Stashes tend to burn holes in your pockets after a few pints here and a few dabs there. We could always score more the next day we told ourselves as we shovelled the lot down. The club was pretty packed, but we knew that the following night would be even busier. All the big-money DJs were on then, and Saturday night is, after all, *the* big club night, generally speaking. After hours of debauchery we emerged from the club, sweaty as you like, eyes like black billiard balls, knowing grins from ear to ear, and waded our way through the thrusting hands of the flyer distributors, telling them not to worry, we were definitely returning the following night. We staggered up the road home, it was only a five-minute walk. And there we stayed up until nine or ten in the morning drinking bourbon, smoking ourselves silly and generally turning the front room into a sea of empty CD cases and bits of Rizla.

When we eventually awoke from a twitchy, restless half-sleep it was around six or seven in the evening. I dragged myself into a sitting position on the edge of the bed, gently trying to convince my brain to let the rest of my body work. When it finally realised that it had no choice – I was going to go out and do it all over again whether it cared to join me or not – it allowed my limbs to start working and I stumbled into the bathroom and ran a bath. And what a glorious bath it was too. My skin tingled as I soaked the remnants of the previous night away. I washed about £294 million packets'-worth of cigarette smoke from my hair and wandered downstairs to see what shape the others were in. Not bad, not bad at all. Someone even managed to cheerfully thrust a cup of tea into my hand. Ah, bliss – tea rules!

The next form of liquid refreshment I gave my poor dehydrated body was a pint down the pub a few hours later, which to be honest didn't go down too well. But by the second and third I was starting to feel almost human again. A very wired human, but human none the less. We tumbled out of the pub, thankfully commenting on the levelling effects of beer, and headed up to the Music Factory to join the very long queue. It didn't seem to take long and we were soon checking our coats in and squeezing our way through to the packed bar. Thinking better of the mobbed downstairs bar we headed upstairs. We knew a load of our mates would be up there anyway. The club was heaving ('on advice from my attorney . . .', as a favourite writer of mine put it, I won't suggest for one minute that the club was quite obviously over-capacity full!) The heat was immense. We battled our way over the dancefloor upstairs to the bar where, sure enough, we were greeted by the gang.

It didn't take us long to score some pills and, after careful deliberation, I decided to take only half – to wait and see what happened. I was still feeling pretty fried. I leaned back on the bar as everyone chatted and knocked the drinks back. I listened and smiled, feeling more like observing than participating. God, it was hot. Even the designer shirts were starting to come off. I remember seeing two girls – they looked identical in their long, silky night dresses, sweat pouring off them as they danced tentatively in their high heels. Ridiculous clubbing attire, high heels! But I won't get into the old 'banned trainer' debate. Come to think of it, nighties are pretty daft clubbing attire too. But hey, they were happy, having fun and hurting no one. My boyfriend,

Alec, decided to pop downstairs with a mate to check out what was going on. I couldn't peel my elbows from the bar behind me so I declined the offer. I stayed to chat with a friend, well actually he chatted, I couldn't bring myself to say much. I couldn't feel any effect from the pill yet, aware only of the fact that the room was getting hotter and hotter (something I apparently kept commenting on – *Is it me or is it getting hotter in here?* I'm told is about all I said to my chatty friend).

Suddenly, I felt the most urgent need to get the hell out of that room. The thought just flashed into my head as my chest began to feel very tight. I told my friend that I was going to go and look for Alec downstairs. He smiled and went off to join the others on the other side of the room where they'd found some seats. I lifted my weight from my elbows and on to my legs and feet. Whoa, wobbly! I started to make my way over the dancefloor to the door to the stairs in the corner. Halfway across it happened; both my eyesight and hearing went completely. I was totally blind and totally deaf. Shit! What the fuck?! I carried on – in my mind's eye I could see that door and all I needed to do was get to it. Then my legs went from under me. I could feel my knees on the floor as my body sagged. I couldn't see any faces or hear any voices, or any music for that matter, but I could feel arms pulling me back to my feet and pushing me past. I don't know whether it was because what I was experiencing was in total darkness and total silence, but I didn't panic. All I remember is one calm thought repeating itself over and over: *This is it. This is what it's like to die on an E. You've done it this time girl. You're dying – alone!*

Somehow, I managed to reach the door and, almost as if I'd swum up from the deepest lake and broken the surface of the water, the cooler air of the main room hit me. I clung on to the rail at the top of the stairs and leaned over, gulping in lungfuls of oxygen. My eyesight and hearing returned partially, enough to see faces in front of me and hear them asking me if I was okay. *Tell them no! Tell them no!* my brain screamed. But my auto-pilot mouth reassured them that I was fine. A bouncer appeared and told me to move away from the rail edge – did I look like I was about to jump? I obliged and turned to see Alec making his way up the stairs. Oh thank fuck! He asked me if I was all right. I told him no, that I needed some air. He turned to follow me down the stairs and looped his arms around my waist. As soon as I felt him holding me something gave. I hardly remember getting down those stairs, but according to Alec, as soon as his arms were around me, my body crumpled. He basically held my whole body up as my legs somehow got me down the stairs and as soon as we hit the last one he couldn't hold me any more. I collapsed – unconscious.

Now I don't remember much about what happened next, being out cold an' all, but he said that he held me and slapped my face and actually thought I was dead. It didn't take long for the bouncers to show up. I had, after all, collapsed very elegantly in my little dress, which was probably by this time up round my ears, in one of the busiest parts of the club. They helped Alec carry me out and I remember coming round and answering their, *Shall we call an ambulance for her, mate?* with an amazing projectile barf. Jumping out of the way just in time, they left Alec to me and my chunder. I looked through wet eyes first down at the puke, then up at his worried, white face and asked him what happened. *How did I get out here?* I whispered. *You collapsed – we carried you out. I thought I'd lost you,* he choked, gripping my trembling hand. I sat there dazed and very confused, repeatedly asking, *How did I get here? What happened?* The only thing I can compare sitting outside that club to, is how you feel when you've come round from an operation, after having a general anaesthetic – watching with numb head through bleary eyes as nurses fuss around you doing nurse-type things. Friends coming out to find us – panicking, then, seeing that I wasn't dead, reluctantly going back inside. I remember hoping that I hadn't spoiled their night.

Alec held on to me tightly as he got me back to our warm, safe house. He got me into my pyjamas and wrapped me up in a duvet on the sofa. We listened to soothing tunes as I sipped the umpteen cups of sweet tea he made me. I didn't say much, just stared straight ahead, contemplating my near-death experience. Maybe it wasn't *that* drastic or serious, but it sure felt like it at the time, and it scared the shit out of both of us. Ironically, I could feel the E working a little; in fact it felt pretty good. *You know,* Alec said, breaking my reverie, *I was downstairs in that club tonight when my E came up and I got the sudden, desperate urge to come and find you and make sure you were okay. I just knew I had to come and get you.* I looked over at him through the steam from my hot tea and I believed him. I believed that he had heard my silent screams from upstairs in that club. What I didn't believe was my reply: *I'm never, ever doing E again.* Yeah right!

Nancy Noble, Sheffield

I've been working as a club bouncer for nearly ten years now.
I've mainly worked in the North: Liverpool, Leeds, Manchester;
I've worked all over. Except Newcastle where the security
business is all sewn up. I've done stints in Edinburgh and
Glasgow, Belfast, Nottingham for a couple of years. I've even
had a couple of jobs abroad, Ibiza for example. I started as a
security guard; there's demand for women as you can go plain-
clothes and you can work in ladies' departments.

You see the other side of the coin when you're a guard. I go out
to clubs sometimes. I know the score, but when you're a punter,
you are against the security; they are just trying to ruin your
night. They are a test you have to get past to get in, they can stop
you going in for no reason if they don't like your face and that's
it, you're out. And you have to get your drugs and sometimes
your chewing gum past them, and hope you're on the guest list
if you've been told you are, and hope you look old enough and
you're wearing the right clothes. So you hate them.

But if there's a ruck they're the first people you blame for letting
undesirables in and the first people you look to to get them out.
People only see the one side of it, they don't see that most of the
bouncers most of the time are looking out for them and for the
club. Apart from a few, most of the security staff I have worked
with aren't against drugs at all and don't want to stop you taking
them. But they have the best interests of the club at heart and
don't want the kind of obvious stupid dealing and drug-taking
that can cause complaints and these days lead to the club being
busted or even shut down. Keep it to yourself, be discreet, be

safe and we don't care. Put the club itself, the promoters or your fellow clubbers at risk and that's where we come in. We are looking at the long-term future of the club so that you can continue to have your nights out. You will complain when it is shut down because the security were allowing blatant dealing to go on inside the club and outside, leading to complaints from locals. That's what happened at UK in Wandsworth, so you know it can happen.

I admit there are some security who shouldn't be in the job, a very small minority who may get off on the power they have over people and who may abuse their position. If this happens, all you have to do is tell the management or the promoters. They don't want their club to have a reputation for unpleasant staff. It isn't good for business. You may think we're stupid when we don't look in your wallet or check your fag packet or ask you to take off your shoes. But we don't always want to find your gear, because a club full of straight people is a shit club, we all know that and that isn't any good for anyone. But don't get us wrong, after you've done club security for a while you can spot the serious dealer from the lad out with his mates and you can spot the straight-up serious dealer from the wanker who's going to be selling shit and putting people at risk.

It's about striking a balance between making sure people are going to have a good time and come back next week and excluding the potential risks. Sometimes you may get it wrong, but I like to be on the safe side myself. I've seen some horrible things from bad drugs or too many drugs cut with shit and so on.

No one wants that, not you, not the promoter, the club owner, management, staff, DJs, or us the security. So we sometimes play it safe. But I think that bad security staff aside, you are the better for it. We don't want to spoil your fun, so work with us. Don't take the piss and we won't either.

Shelley

Max and Ivan stumble from the relative quiet of the toilet straight into the brunt of the ferociously loud and sweaty main dancefloor. Midnight has passed without them realising. It's now 1990. A powerful strobe flashes hard blankets of light into the faces of the dancers. Ugly twisted faces appear for a split-second only to be swallowed up again by the black mass of the warehouse.

A juddering sub-bass slides up and down. A sampled voice gasps, *What's wrong with these people?* For Max the question is incredibly apt and timely. He can see a difference. The smiles and friendliness seem to have been replaced by a harsh desperation, a huffing and puffing determination to dance all night, not for the love of it but because of frustration and amphetamine overload. There's been a change in the people. The music and vibe are no longer the most important; it's the drugs.

The sound suddenly cuts out. A moan goes up from the throng. Max slows down and realises he's lost Ivan. A burst of deafening feedback pierces the sudden lull. Everyone bounces gently as if on big rubber space-hoppers. Sucking on imaginary golf-balls, their faces are flushed a blotchy red. On the makeshift stage a shadowy figure taps a microphone.

Hello? his deep voice rumbles over the quietly droning system. *Look. There's loads of people outside trying to get in. What we've done is lock the doors to make sure that no one else forces their way in. Don't panic.*

Someone sprays CS gas and everyone bustles in all directions. There is mayhem as people push and shove wildly. That telling sample echoes around Max's strained brain, *What's wrong with these people?* He aims himself to go with the surging flow. Someone slips and takes a bundle of people down with them. Screams and cries peal out.

Luckily, Max manages to clamber out of the way and reach the side of the warehouse. His eyes and nostrils sting from the sharp gas as it disperses throughout the room. He looks for any sign of Ivan. Everyone's face is full of fear and panic. Every fleeting expression is totally insane. The heat is almost unbearable.

Next to him some bloke starts smashing a pane of glass in a small window. The bloke squeezes himself through, ripping his clothes, hands and knees in the process. Max hesitantly creeps over to have a look. After briefly attempting to make sure that no sharp splinters of glass are sticking out, he pulls himself up carefully. He rips his dungarees and purple top severely and cuts his finger.

Once outside, however, he feels a lot better instantly. The cool air and space are heaven-sent. He leans against a crumbly wall and tries to calm down. The night has been a total nightmare and it's not over yet. Strangled screams and wails continue to drift out of the warehouse.

People are milling around but keep their heads down as they disperse swiftly, obviously freaked out by the whole affair.

Behind a mountainous, gleaming office block and various gangly, stranded cranes, the sun wanly struggles up. The lame grey light, however, lifts some of the violence of the night. Max gazes morosely at the devastating rip in his beloved dungarees.

To his intense relief, Max comes across a couple he knows from Southend. Nick and Josie are a bit older, in their mid-twenties and very hippyfied. They've been selling fruit from a stall in the rave. *Am I glad to see someone I know*, exclaims Max cheerfully. *Jesus, what a nightmare this has been. Tell me about it*, replies Nick grumpily. *It's a fucking war zone. This will go down in history as the most unpleasant experience of my life so far.* Nervously pawing the top of his chest, Nick recounts what happened to them. *I was just standing there, waiting for me next customer, right? When this lanky bloke comes over and demands me crystals. I always keep 'em round me neck for good karma y'know.* His hands twitch around his bare throat. *When I refused he got out a great big knife, leant over and cut through the rope. I fuckin' cacked me pants. That weirded us out so much we decided to get out. It wasn't easy, I tell ya. Shit man, you should have seen the pushing and shoving going on outside. The two blokes on the door looked off it, really struggling. Did you see that dog? Mad.*

They all gang around Nick and Josie's dilapidated little fruit van, keeping an eye out for their various missing mates. Max takes some comfort from just being with people he knows. *Get in the back of the van*, offers Nick. *It can get a bit cold in there so wrap yourself up in that blanket.*

Max gratefully clambers into the fruit van. Once the stiff door is slammed firmly shut and the outside world is locked out, a flood of relief pours over him. He suddenly feels so old, as if the strain of the night has prematurely aged him. Just then, Nick and Josie snap the front doors open and start the van quickly. *Pigs*, spits Nick. *Let's split before we're hassled.*

Max rolls around the back of their refrigerated van between loose oranges, melons and a large sour apple, a thick and rough grey blanket wrapped around his shoulders. The van wobbles into a garage and Max peers out of the dust-encrusted back window. *Is that a line of geezers with their hands on their hips?* he wonders out loud. Josie turns back to him and smiles warmly, *No love, they're the petrol pumps.* She skins up on the dashboard whilst waiting for Nick. He bundles back in, clutching chocolate biscuits, crisps, chewing gum and fruit juice.

Back on the road they decide to head for Clapham Common. It has become quite a tradition for ravers to congregate there on a

Sunday and there's a chance they may meet up with some of their lost compadres.

Lying back on uncomfortable lumps of fresh fruit, Max sucks down the thick black smoke. It has no discernible effect on him. Gazing at the scratches on the roof of the little van, Max listens to Nick and Josie getting increasingly stressed as they go down various one-way systems the wrong way.

By the time they arrive at Clapham Common, the morning is miserable, depressingly grey and rainy. Splitting up, they resolve to meet back at the van in an hour's time. Max holds the borrowed horsehair blanket close, trying to keep out the biting wind and lashing rain. Because of the nasty weather there aren't many people about. Max wanders aimlessly into a perpetual grey void, the unlikely chance of finding Ivan driving him forwards. Through the sheen of grey drizzle a lone colourful figure stalks towards him. As it gets closer, Max recognises it as a friendly bloke they'd chatted to several times at various raves and parties. *'Ere mate!* Max grins, tears of accumulated rain dribbling down his face. *Yo! Have you seen one of my mates?* Ignoring Max steadfastly, the rained-on geezer keeps his head down and carries on walking. His hunted eyes flit this way and that but avoid Max. He is stiff with paranoia.

For fuck's sake, groans Max, *what is wrong with everyone today?* He is again reminded of that telling sample which seemed to sum up the blank aggressive vibe of the rave. *Happy fucking New Year*, he mutters.

Before too long Max is soaked to the bone. A sluggish come-down and kick-back from the overwhelming stress of the night starts to creep up on him. With the rough blanket wrapped tightly around him and his boots squelching with every step, he feels like a complete tramp. Lacking a watch he doesn't know when to go back to see if Nick and Josie are waiting for him at the van and can't bring himself to ask anyone the time. He keeps holding out, vainly hoping that the next person he passes will be Ivan.

When he finally gets back to the place where the van had been parked, he finds it's gone. This is just the icing on the cake, overstepping the limits of his panic and despair. He plods around thinking they might be waiting for him somewhere else but eventually comes to the conclusion that they've buggered off. Plucking up the courage, he asks a passer-by the time and finds out that it's nearly two hours since they split up. Nick and Josie must have got fed up with waiting and gone. He digs twenty-five pence out of his pockets. *That's not right,* he thinks. *I must have lost some.* Great.

It's not enough for the Tube or the bus, although he's still got his British Rail card, so his only option is to walk to Fenchurch Street, on the other side of London.

The journey takes him three hours. The most unpleasant bit is walking through the City and feeling so small and dirty compared to the huge intimidating bank buildings. It also reminds him that he's got work tomorrow; back into his suit and tie, hair slicked back. Maybe he could ring up and say he's ill and can't come in. He certainly feels ill.

On the jolting train, he scrunches himself into a ball, shattered and shivering. He can't bear anyone looking at him so he pulls the sodden blanket completely over his head.

Once he finally gets home Max tries to run straight upstairs but his mum has been waiting and corners him in the hall. *Where the hell have you been, young man? We've been worried sick! I, err, got split up from Ivan*, Max replies. *I was trying to find him all over London*. He tries a few sneaky moves towards the stairs. *Where have you been then? Talk to me; where have you been?* she asks. *Can I have a bath first, Mum? I feel really mucky. Remember you've got work tomorrow*, calls his step-dad from the living room.

Thankfully, Max is allowed to go upstairs unhindered. His mother watches him go sharply. *Well, you must have had a good time to stay out all night and day*, she calls up to his bowed back.

If only she knew, he thinks wearily. *If only she knew . . .*
Daniel Newman, London

The last thing they were, was good freakin' shit.

When I said fifteen for three, the guy nearly choked on his Red Stripe, but there was no way I was going to pay eighteen quid for each of 'em, no way. So I says, *C'mon mate, forty-five quid for three*, and this time he looks at us and says, *Wait a minute, I'll see what I can do*. He walks over to some bird with long blonde hair by the bar, has a word with her, then walks back. *Okay,* he says, *come with me into the bogs. It's too chancy out here with the fuckin' bouncers an' that.*

We walked into the bogs and it was packed, full of the usual people talking about fuck knows what. In here, he says, pointing to a cubicle, so in we go.

Next thing that happens is two other lads open the door and squeeze in and I looked at 'em all and realised something was up.

Hey, what's the score?

You are, mate, my dealer says. *Get your fuckin' Lacoste sweater off for starters!*

You what? One of the other lads gets out a knife and sticks it to me throat.

Get the fucking sweater off! Get your money out and your dope.

I haven't got any dope.

Shut the fuck up and do it. We know you've got dope 'cos we've been watching you smoke it all fuckin' night. So I took me sweater off, 150 quids' worth, and hands it to 'em. Then he sees me Burberry shirt. *Off!*

You what?! The lad sticks the knife closer, so I take off me shirt. *Empty your pockets.* I do, giving 'em 130 quid and a quarter of dope. Then they looks at me Timberland boaters. *Off. You what?!* As soon as I say that, the lad takes the knife and slashes me elbow, fuckin' really hurting me, blood spitting crimson everywhere, so I take me Timberlands off. *Right. Your jeans. They're Armani, aren't they? Take the fuckers off!* he says, grinning at me with the knife in hand. I take the Armanis off. Then he notices me boxer-shorts. Calvin Kleins. *Off.*

You what?!

Take 'em off, now! Let's see what's for breakfast! So off come the Calvins, and he gets 'em on the end of the fuckin' knife and holds 'em up like a flag, his two mates laughing their heads off. Then he bungs 'em into the next cubicle, gets the knife, makes me turn round and sticks it right up me arsehole, telling me to keep it shut or else.

Then they're gone, and I'm left there, sprawled over the bog, crimson rushing from me arse, and the pain's unbearable. It's the motherfucker of all agony, and I'm breathing too fast, everything's beginning to blur, and I slide down off the bog and lie there on the floor of the cubicle, and just as I'm beginning to pass out, these two monster fuckin' eyes, like black stones frying in egg whites, appear under the partition, and then there's a mouth and it's saying:

Snowy. Get 'em from Snowy. White New Yorkers. Fuckin' powder pills. Good shit man, good shit . . .

And then I passed out.

Until now that is.

I came round and some ambulance guy was looking at me and I could hear the sirens and the road rushing past outside.
Jamie Jackson, London

It hit her the same time as it hit me; I could see it. It was like walking into a wall: amazing. You know how it feels when the rush is almost too much to bear and you don't know whether to close your eyes in case you explode or dance like a dervish? I looked at her: I'm just going up to the chill-out room for a bit, she said. I hoped she would be able to handle it: pills had never affected her at all before and we had decided to give them one last chance before she gave up.

But this one affected her. Over the next twenty minutes I struggled to hold it together as I saw her drifting away from me and begin sledging, despite how hard I could see her fighting it. Perhaps that made it worse, I don't know. She told me later she could hear me telling her, Come on, try to look at me, try to breathe, I love you, come on. *But she just couldn't move. Her consciousness was slipping and her eyes rolled back in their sockets; then she seemed to stop breathing.*

I don't know how I got her out of that room, so packed you had to pick your way over legs and arms and prone bodies. I wasn't in a much better state than she was, although I hadn't had the base she had been dipping into all evening before deciding, Fuck it, *and dropping the pill. We were halfway down the stairs that seemed to go on forever, me shouting for a medic, when suddenly she moved. It was like a current going through her body: her muscles jerked, she looked up at me, and her eyes were clear and focused.*

We spent the rest of that night on the stairs. She looked very small, very shaken, and still very scared. She kept apologising for making me miss Laurent Garnier, but I didn't care. Despite everything, I had the best night out, because I got her back.
Anon

Energy II: Heston, June 1989: By the time we got there the police had blocked the road and there were thousands of people trying to get in. I was with my brother, Tim, and we thought the event had been stopped until some bright spark said, *There are people in there! You can hear them!* So I went up to the police and told them that this was a private party, we had tickets, and they couldn't stop us going in. When they refused, I asked to speak to whoever was in charge, but I was told he was at the station and if I wanted to go there he'd be happy to see me. This I wasn't going to do, so I suggested that they get everyone in line and check they had tickets, start policing it sensibly because there was some good press in it for them. But they weren't having it. *All you people want to do is take drugs,* said one policeman. *We're not taking drugs!* I protested, wide-eyed. *We're here to dance!* And then some raver staggers up, completely off his head, saying, *Drugs? Drugs? No mate, no one here's on drugs, no drugs here mate . . .*

Eventually, someone suggested storming a wall that we could see was the only obstacle between us and the party we had paid to attend and had every right to be at. So we all ran towards the wall, me and my brother and a whole bunch of people, and suddenly the police were everywhere, some of them in riot gear, and I looked back and everyone was heading the other way! It wasn't until I was back in amongst the crowds that I realised I didn't know where my brother was; as it went, we weren't going to see him that night. So we found our way back to the car, not knowing if he'd been arrested, or got lost, or where he was.

We did get in eventually, although a lot of people gave up and went home because they thought it wasn't going to happen. A couple of police vans nearly got turned over whilst we were waiting, and cans and bottles did get thrown. A crowd on E is not a hostile crowd by nature, but you can't keep people out when they want to get in, have travelled and paid to get in, and have every right (or had in those days) to get in. Eventually, the police realised that. In any case, they were not in control of the crowd, who had started to invade people's gardens in the surrounding area in a bid to find a way in. Local people had started phoning the police saying they had twenty kids in their garden, but the police were already there, and eventually they realised it was a lot less hassle to just let the people party.

I spent most of the night looking for Tim, who I was sure had been arrested. Sometimes when you're on an E and something isn't quite right, it's hard to ignore. You dance for a bit, but you can't really get into it until you've put it right. You feel restless until you've found your mates, or remembered what it was you wanted to say, or satisfied yourself that the guy in the corner really is okay. We discovered afterwards that he'd got over the fence and been in there all along, we'd just never seen him.

Simon, London

This should have been the best night out ever. If you had asked me on Saturday morning what I was doing that night, I would have waxed lyrical about the delights awaiting me and my three cohorts at the club they call Nosebleed. I would have bragged about how I got our names on the guest list, and that we would get to interview the great Temper Tantrum and Nasenbluten. However, if you had asked me on Sunday afternoon what I had done on Saturday night, I would have simply said, *Don't ask!*

On arriving in Rosyth, we knew that things were going to go wrong because we found the venue practically straight away. Normally, we would be fashionably late to these things, because the venues are so damn underground, and hence hard to find. But there it was, clear as day, or as clear as day can be through my mate's strangely steamed up square Nissan. It must have been the rapidly building excitement, or crap heater, or something. I was deeply perturbed by the legend attached to the venue: 'Visions – Lounge Bar'. The idea of one of the most notorious hardcore clubs being held in a lounge bar did not bode well. Needless to say, finding the place so bloody quickly also meant that we had arrived too early. To kill time we sent one of our little gang out on a reccy to make sure that we were at the right place, and that some big joke was not about to befall us. He returned almost too quickly, and confirmed our worst fears.

Suddenly, as if by magic, people appeared. We had to laugh. Total ned-fest. There were the trendies, the ravers, the clubbers, and slappers to name but four. Like Stepford wives, the birds all looked the same: short skirts and crop-tops, or tracksuit bottoms and crop-tops, trying to achieve the 'Sporty Spice' look. The blokes were just as bad. The gabba scene has certainly done a lot for the dwindling shell-suit market. It was at this point we dared to get out of the car, push our way to the front of the queue, and get in using that infamous line, *It's all right, we're on the guest list.*

We were not. I saw the guest list, and our names were not down. We were not coming in. Surprisingly, the door staff were dead friendly and went off to find out what the story was. They came back a bit later and said that we would have to wait for the person we were supposed to meet from Earache. The wait began. We waited so long in fact that about ten minutes later it was just us and the bouncers standing by the draughty door. Before I had an uncontrollable fit, the friendly lady bouncer went off to find the promoter. He arrived on the scene and a shouty conversation ensued, where it came to pass that there had been some breakdown in communication, meaning that only two names were down on some list somewhere. He spelled out our options: four people could come in, but two would have to pay, or we could all fuck off.

Once inside, it was clear that there was no backstage area as such, as the backstage area was literally the stage, so any interviews we might have done would have been inaudible anyway. I was also lumbered with my lovely heavy record bag. Fortunately, having the record bag provided some entertaining moments, with the natives thinking that I was one of the PAs. *Are you a PA?* they quizzed. *No,* I replied, *I'm with a magazine. M8?* they incorrectly assumed. *No, InnerSpace.* The blank look of non-recognition said it all. I also wondered why having a record bag made you a PA. A DJ perhaps, but not a PA. I know electrical equipment is getting smaller all the time, but did they really expect me to be able to fit all the necessary gabba-making technology into an XL record bag? Apparently so.

It was whilst hammering the air to DJ Jackhammer that I had a revelation. I noticed that, like the recipe for a disaster movie, the ingredient characters were present for this disaster evening. You know the sort of movies I mean. The ones that are repeated ad infinitum every Christmas, Easter and other religious festivals, where the same characters appear, almost sensing the danger ahead. There was the smartly-dressed old married couple whose marriage may or may not be on the rocks; the nutters who cannot handle the pressure and are easily recognisable because they are unable to dance properly, preferring to spin and jump about like whirling dervishes; and the pregnant woman. I mean I ask you, who in their right mind would take a pregnant woman to a hard as hell gabba club? I was almost expecting the inevitable faithless priest to appear, and try to convert us gabbers into new wave Christian fundamentalists, whilst reaffirming his own faith, when my flow of thought was interrupted by one of my cohorts, who pointed out that the girls with the teasingly almost-see-through clothes on had overcome the problem of white underwear showing through in the UV light by not wearing any. This was something I tried to find out as the evening went on. I came to the conclusion that he had made this story up, as most of the girls I saw seemed to be wearing their underwear as clothes.

For the rest of the evening we counted our losses (about ten) and went mental on the dancefloor to some excellent gabba sounds, something I have not done since those halcyon days of club '23', in Edinburgh.

Tim Veale, Guildford

Jesus Streaky, you look fucked! He did too. Very. *I've had three Es, a gram of speed and a purple Om,* he said.

Joe (Streaky to his mates) was in a right state. It was always the same. Whenever we went raving, Joe had to take more drugs than anyone else. Just had to. Tonight though he looked worse than usual. He'd been selling pills for his brother and by my reckoning he'd taken more than he'd sold. *What I did, right*, he spluttered, *was put a Dennis the Menace, two New Yorkers, the whizz and the trip in a bomb and necked it in one. I'm off my nut!* This was the understatement of the year. His face looked as though it had been put through a mangle and would need hospital treatment to put it back to normal. Not a pretty sight. His pupils were so dilated that there was no colour to his normally blue eyes, just huge, staring black pools. Scary. *Joe, I've got to go home, mate*. There was no way I was going to get any sense out of this headcase. More to the point, looking at his ugly mug was starting to affect my own buzz. The rushes were starting to subside and I could feel myself falling back to Earth. *Catch later, geez.*

Hardcore. That's what I needed. *Fuckin' 'ardcore!* The hairs on the back of my neck began to bristle and a huge sense of anticipation washed over me as I made my way back to the main room. What had I gone outside for in the first place?

Much like any other rave, it was murder trying to find your mates in the Tasco warehouse and a headful of chemicals didn't help. Not to worry. I was having a blinder by myself, dancing about all over the place, shaking people's hands and jabbering enthusiastically.

Some time passed. It may have been a couple of minutes or an hour or so. No idea. What I was beginning to realise was that I was becoming over-stimulated. To put it another way, I was starting to lose it badly. Time for a lean I reckoned. There was no way I was going to risk a sit-down. In the state I was in I'd probably spend the rest of the night on my arse, stuck in some corner of the chill-out room with my eyes in the back of my head. Sod that. I'd spent the best part of a two-week giro on tonight and I wasn't going to let it degenerate into that.

Making my way tentatively to where some pillars lined the back of the warehouse, I kept getting huge whiffs of different types of ganja. Shit, I needed a joint. Trying not to bump into too many people or trample on too many feet, I finally found a free pillar to prop myself up against. Shit. I really needed a joint. I just couldn't seem to focus on anyone I could pester for a few tokes.

Things were starting to get a bit much here. I could feel my jaw going. My eyes were starting to roll and I knew I'd be on the deck if I didn't have something to support me. Oh shit.

Take it.

Eh?

Take it, (louder).

What the fuck was going on here? Opening my eyes and trying

to make sense of my surroundings, I could see a big red pulsating object burning away right in front of my face. What the . . . ?

Mesmerised by the sight, it took a third *Take it!* for me to realise that it was a spliff. Someone had seen the state of me and was offering me a joint. *Yes!*

Cheers mate, I gurned pathetically. It was all I could muster. The big rasta who had come to my rescue disappeared, laughing, leaving me and my prize. Skunk! Result!

Taking a few tokes, the mayhem in my mind started to lessen. I was still wasted, but beginning to gain some control over my situation. Heartened by this, I tried to get back into the swing of things with a few moves but my legs weren't having any of it. Temporarily admitting defeat, I decided to try to track down some of my mates in the chill-out room.

Winding my way back through the dancefloor, I could feel my drugs working together, unified by the skunk. This was intense. Channelling my way past the cloakroom and the bar, I eventually made it. Attempting not to tread on too many of the overheated ravers who were scattered all over the rave, I did a quick search. There all by himself in a world of his own was Whirly – trying to make a joint but failing miserably.

I just can't get the skins to stick together man. His pupils were huge and, unsurprisingly, he couldn't focus on the Rizlas. Even holding them at arm's length. *Whirl, where's Matt?* I asked. *Just gone back inside with John, geez. They've just had another rhubarb and custard each.*

Later man. Scouring the outer podiums first, just in case, I finally found Matt and John at the front of the main stage. *John, geez!* I shouted. *Richy! Up here son!* Grabbing his arm, I somehow scrambled on to the stage. *Here* he said. Another rhubarb and custard? Surely not! Fuck it. *Cheers John.*

There I was then. There was nothing for it but to try to crank my legs back into action. This time they worked. Overjoyed, the hands went in the air, and that's about the last thing I remember.
Rich Jones, Kingston

1993 was a weird year. It was the year when the scene began to go into the clubs, when we first sensed that the party was over but didn't know what was to come. The big outdoor spectacles were happening less and less, attendances were down and it was getting harder and harder in a hostile media spotlight to put on the sort of parties we had been going to. There was a hiatus between the rave scene coming to an end and the club scene taking off: the commercial, expensive nightlife that's taken over the cities and produced the formula music you hear on every ad. It was like the moment after all the fireworks have gone off when you stand there still looking at the sky, just before you put your hands in your pockets and go home.

Some people call what's happened to music since the heady

days of house 'diversification'. I call it commercialisation, fragmentation. The scene is split now, where it used to be united. It's all about money and marketing: opening the club, releasing the mix CD, getting the kids to wear the clothes, carry the bag, pay the price. About declaring their allegiance to one schism or the other. The bad times are now, and most clubbers don't even know it. They think what they're doing is exciting and revolutionary, but they're being manipulated by capitalism, just puppets in the hands of the money-makers, allowing themselves to be contained and restricted, letting themselves be satisfied with glitter and noise and fluff, moving inescapably towards a placid and conventional adulthood like the soldiers who were fed bromide in the First World War.

The rave years were an experiment in anarchy, and they worked. Some of the big events ran for days like self-organising states; no one could have stopped them or taken charge. But nothing went wrong; on the whole, people looked after each other because it was in our interests to do so. Thousands of like-minded people came together to do one thing: dance. Trouble, when it came, came from the authorities. Because they were scared, because this thing was bigger than them. People weren't frightened of them any more; they weren't aggressive towards them either, just indifferent. And indifference is a terrible thing to authority.

We grew up without a lot of the things our parents took for granted. We grew up in a society that was, and is, fundamentally unstable. We grew up with the reality of widespread unemployment and job insecurity, with a soaring divorce rate and growing poverty. We have no community of our own, so we made one: a community of clubbers. It's still there in the clubs today, for you can't stamp it out; it's needed too much. It's about family, about trusting the people you're with, about security and identity. We didn't step into a world where those things were there for us, so we made them. And that's what makes the dance music phenomenon different from Punk for example, or the New Romantics. It's about more than music or clothes or the drugs which the media love to publicise. It's about finding a common identity and a culture to call our own.

K, Glasgow

We had decided to escape to Thailand for a couple of months as our lifestyle in London was starting to get the better of us. To celebrate our departure to a chilled-out beach, we went partying full-on for two weeks. During this time I had two of the scariest moments of my life but they didn't seem like moments at the time, more like bloody years!

I think it all started at the beginning of the party fortnight. That Saturday, Andy and I called Kath in Camden and then Kath and I went for a pint in Covent Garden while Andy went off to buy a new mixer. *I'm glad we took it easy last night and got a good night's sleep. Tonight and Sunday are going to be mad and no doubt we'll be in 828 on Monday morning* I said. *That goes without saying. I'm not letting you's two to Thailand without a wicked weekend* she replied.

The three of us arrived at The Sanctuary around two p.m. and everyone was there. We had organised the party about three weeks ago so the word had spread. After greeting everyone, Kath and I went to the loos looking for our favourite dealer. There was no one in them except this seedy creep. No matter how seedy he looked, when he offered us some charley we went into the cubicle with him, no problem. After a big fat line each we tried to go, but Creepy was having none of it. He was right in thinking that after a couple of smokes of crack we would be more relaxed.

It was the first time I had smoked the stuff and bloody hell was it good or what? We were both lying up against the wall floating in pink clouds. We came back down with a bump when we realised what was going on. Earlier we gave Creepy £50 for a gram and now he wasn't going to let us out of the loo unless Kath and I performed. It was at this stage that I had it all worked out what I was going to do when he pulled the knife. He was wired. After a lot of sweet-talking, some shouting and then more pleading when we saw the reaction to raised voices we worked out a deal with him. Kath was going out to get more money for him and he was going to look after me till she came back. Boy, I was quaking in my trainers. Kath came back all right, but not with the money, with the boys. Did I feel like a pathetic female or what, getting rescued like a damsel.

Anyway, we recovered enough to party hard. Our party was a stormer and on Sunday night we were still up. Coming out of Self Indulgence the natural thing to do was to go to 828 and finish in style. Before we left, Andy bought three more pills so we were sorted. Driving down to Brixton we came across a police checkpoint.

Shit.

Richard and I sat in the car motionless as Andy dealt with the coppers. He kept his cool and gave them the right answers, so we drove on without trouble – or so we thought. *Wow, you handled that well!* we congratulated Andy. *I was crapping myself. I took those three pills in my pocket before I got out* he replied. *What, you triple dropped? Oh shit!*

None of us had double dropped never mind triple, so I started to get quite worried. We parked, went into the club and Richard and I kept a close eye on Andy. Within forty-five minutes of dropping, it was obvious something big was happening to him. His legs went like jelly and also his mind. Nothing was connecting so we took him outside and placed him in the car. I was frightened out of my mind but tried to keep calm as someone had to be in control. I have never in my entire clubbing lifetime seen someone so out of it but still conscious. We had to drive to Oxford that morning as we had promised to get people home, and Andy was the only one insured on the car. He insisted he was fine but we knew he wasn't. Driving to Oxford on the M40 was one of the hairiest moments ever. I was coming down badly and I had to steer the car along the motorway, as Andy had no concept of lanes or other cars. I really think I should have a head of grey hair after that morning. We dropped people off in

Oxford and then drove back to London. Thinking back it was such a stupid thing to even get into the car but at the time we thought we had no choice. Driving back, my nerves were shattered, screaming every time we nearly missed another car.

Okay, you drive, I was told. So I drove back to London. I hadn't slept in three days and was full of drugs and drink. It was a miracle we reached home in one piece.

After that weekend I have realised that drugs do take your life away and am trying to give up totally. We found out that the pills were Ketamine and Andy has blanked out a week of his life. He doesn't remember anything after the police checkpoint. Maybe that's not a bad thing.
Val Wylie, Edinburgh

Have you noticed, in films, how the action always cuts from one location to another. The actors are in a house in Edinburgh, they are seen jumping into a car and – cut – they arrive at their destination in London. That version of time, all the interesting bits with the mind-numbingly slow pace of the stuff in between cut out, is what differentiates the fantasy of films from the second by second slog of the real life.

So DJing at more than one club on a night looks like a good idea on paper, two club names are written down on a date in the diary. They look pretty close together on the big map. There's a nice big motorway connecting the two and the promise of the double money more than balances out the thought of the bit of extra travelling, anyway Rori's going to be driving, all I have to do is sit there . . .

But in practice, with the added unforeseeable element of some very, very thick soupy fog, the night becomes little more than one whitewashed-out, sleepy but terrifying car journey with little flashes of bright lights and hot, sweaty bodies moving to house music in between. Each minute becomes a potentially deadly drift through a nebulous black and white world. A white line, phantom tail-lights and near-invisible signs saying, *In case of fog read this* . . . Then it's gone. *In case of fog read this* . . . Was that it or was there more? If there was what did it say? *In case of fog read this* . . . *there's a dead end with a 2,000 metre drop into a pit just up the road, you'd better stop now or. . . ? In case of fog read this* . . . *watch out because it's a bit foggy so don't go too fast?* Okay, or just, *In case of fog read this* . . . *weird, isn't it?* Was that our turning or . . . yes, it was, I think. I'm not sure any more. Stop, reverse. Are you sure you can do this on motorways in the fog? Oh my God. Cut to club, cut to club. No, it won't happen because this is the real life not the nightlife and definitely not a good way to make a living.

Dash – dash – dash, the white lines flash, and eventually the first club comes into view, a concrete blob that would be a blot on the landscape if we could see the landscape. In through the door, there's the dancefloor with . . . Oh God, let me out, back into the fog, the uncertainties of the night. Now I wish the fog reached inside too, because there must be fifty people in the club and twenty on the dancefloor and fifteen of them definitely work here, and the other five are just walking across it with their coats on, on their way out of the door. Still, heads down, the records spin, the monitor is an old bass guitar amp but who cares, fifty more minutes and we're out of here, slam, bam, mixed that one okay – just. If you crouch down, fingers on the faders, head below the desk, ear to the speaker, you can almost stop the sound of the treble reverberating round the empty shell and . . . Last record, zip, bags packed, cool, bye, back into the fog bank, bang.

Another hour and a half of drift, half life, white lines go on for ever, keep your eyes on the road. God, I want to go home. *Pronto, si, va bene*. Rori is on the phone. The other club is full (yes!). There's someone at the motorway exit to guide us through the, no, there's no fog either, a pocket of clear, clean air in the middle of this mess (yes!) Maybe this story will have a happy ending after all.

Roll into club number two, the car park's packed, there's steam coming out of that open door and blam, inside, up on to a stick with a little walkway that looks like an Olympic beacon, overlooking a sea of out and happy dancers, zip, click, the record spins, bounce, kick, this is what it's all about. This is why we've been driving all night . . . THIS is the nightlife.

Christopher Mellor, DJ Magazine, London

I'm not what you might call a medic as I don't work for a club and wear a fluorescent jacket. But I go to clubs with one or two other first-aiders to make sure people are safe of a weekend. It's volunteer work and you have to have had training and know what to do, and you have to be a certain type of person and not pass judgement or be shocked. It's not everyone's cup of tea, but I find it more rewarding than the first-aiding I used to do because although I am not young any more (fifty-four) I love the music and I like to be at the clubs with the clubbers and be part of it.

I think it's terribly exciting what is happening now. I have been clubbing when I have not been on duty and I find everyone is very friendly and very positive towards older people. They seem to like to see their parents' generation sharing what they have made for themselves, even if they would not like to see their actual parents there!

I have seen some nasty cases, as you can imagine. Mostly it comes from people not knowing what the drugs they are taking will do if they have not taken them before, or just not being sensible about it. Also, people taking more than they usually would out of bravado or if they think something isn't working and then take more. I always tell people they should be drinking about a pint of water an hour if they have taken ecstasy or amphetamines, but to sip it slowly. They should take regular breaks from dancing and seek help if they feel at all unwell, mentally or physically. It's also better not to mix drugs at all, although we are finding that people are tending to do this more and more now. It is also very important for them to tell the medical staff what they have taken if they become unwell. Patient confidentiality means they will not get in trouble. In any case, our priority is their recovery and we cannot look after them properly if they or their friends are not honest with us. We are not here to pass judgement; we know what goes on, and we just want to make sure you are safe.

I have not seen anyone die at a club and I hope I never do. What a terrible waste it would be of any young life and how terrible for the person's friends they are with. So please be safe whatever you're doing, and don't take risks with your drugs. No drugs are worth dying for after all.

Anon

history in the making

Sunrise, White Waltham, 24 June 1989: We'd all got our tickets in advance and we headed out on to the M4. The directions were given on a series of phone lines; you were directed to a certain place, say a service station, and then you called for the next set. I remember thinking to myself that I had never seen so many cars – as far as you could see there were lights. Nothing was coming into London, but hundreds and hundreds of cars were leaving London in a great convoy, a river of red tail-lights stretching ahead for what looked like miles.

Eventually, we got to the turn-off and found ourselves suddenly in a village side-road. The gardens of the houses came right down to the road, and the road was bumper to bumper with cars. There were people standing in their gardens in their pyjamas and looking out of their windows in their dressing-gowns, wondering what the hell was going on: the sleepy village road suddenly had cars three abreast, all packed with sweaty, gurning kids with their music pumping. Nothing could have come the other way even if it had wanted to.

We got to the bottom of the road and found it was the entrance to an airfield. Then we saw the security: heavy black guys with pit bulls and huge torches, as usual, but in dickie bows! I knew then it was going to be a memorable night.

There was a huge queue to get inside the main hangar. The security were patrolling the queue saying, *Don't sell your drugs out here, sell them inside . . . don't sell your drugs out here, sell them inside . . .* I remember walking in and just thinking, *Fucking*

history in the making

hell! It was a huge hangar, absolutely massive, with big spheres hanging from the roof which were being used as screens to project images on to – some trippy, some downright scary. There was what looked like a tube strung from the roof which ran the whole length of the building with pulsing lights and lasers, fire-eaters, unbelievably huge dance platforms and towers . . . it was incredible. And at some point during a really amazing, mad night, I remember thinking, *This is a Sunrise event. I wonder if I'll see the sun rise . . . I wonder if they'll open the doors . . .* and at about five in the morning, sure enough, the doors began to swing back. These doors were huge, the height of the whole aircraft hangar, and by the time they had finally opened, it seemed to me that everyone inside was facing them, watching for the sunrise, waiting to see what was happening outside.

And there, silhouetted in the door, were two tiny figures. And even against the increasing daylight we could make out that they were uniformed coppers, and that each of them was holding a push bike! They left the bikes there and began to walk slowly into the hangar, and as they came in we could see that one of them was middle-aged and the other was a young guy, perhaps in his twenties. And the younger one had his helmet under his arm, and he wandered in looking totally gobsmacked – they had obviously never seen anything like it in their whole careers of policing a tiny, sleepy, suburban village. And as they passed one of the dance platforms, surrounded on all sides by drugged-up ravers, someone leaned down to the younger copper, gave him his hand, and gave him a lift up on to the platform! So he's standing there, smiling, not quite sure what to do, and he might have stayed there but someone on one of the higher levels of the platform leant down and stuck a bottle of poppers under his nose, which completely freaked him out.

But there were no problems with the police at the event itself, which carried on until mid-morning. But the papers the next day were full of pictures of gurning, sweating people on the dance platforms, with bizarre, alarmist headlines, blowing it all totally out of proportion.
Simon, London

Early 1994 saw the first few outdoor parties which would go on to develop into a major scene across Japan. I was out there in May staying with an English friend of mine called Tom, who lives in Kyoto, and was lucky enough to attend one of the first and biggest.

At that time there wasn't much of a club scene in the regional cities like Kyoto, Nagoya, Osaka; you were lucky if you found one of what we at that time would call a proper club, with perhaps one, maybe two more venues that could be used as club spaces from time to time when foreign or big-name Japanese DJs visited.

It was the second time I'd been to Japan and I'd been out there for ten days or so, when we began to hear about this outdoor party on the following Saturday. The publicity was fairly underground and low-key: photocopied flyers with a rough location somewhere near Omachi and a unicorn logo; but most of it was word-of-mouth and friend-of-a-friend. We knew about thirty people who were going up there – Aussies, Canadians, Americans and a handful of New Zealanders as well as the Japanese kids who were into dance music – and we knew of most of the DJs, who were all Japanese. It was a bit like the scene in England in '88; you knew roughly what to expect but there wasn't anything like the exposure you get now because it was still underground, and it was a fairly small community of people who were organising and attending the events.

There were four of us going: me, Tom, and two Japanese girls who were friends of Tom's. We set off at about 8pm and drove the first 250k or so from Kyoto on main roads, then turning off onto what I suppose in Britain would be 'B' roads for about another 60k. The interior of Japan is mountainous and fairly wild and, although there are a few motorways across it, it's a big untamed space. And this party was a long, long way from any of the major conurbations.

Needless to say, by midnight we were completely lost. After driving around on these crazy little roads in the mountains in the dark for a while, we finally sussed out that the directions printed on the flyer in English were different to the directions printed in Japanese – and I mean totally different, taking us down different roads in totally different directions. It was obvious that two separate people had written both sets, probably from different maps.

To add to all this, it was pissing down – as hard as you ever see rain fall. And it had been like this all the way. We were sitting at the side of the road, drinking cans of beer and smoking a spliff, and not that far from giving up when we spotted it.

Next to the car was an old, faded, flaky sign pointing up this little mud track up the side of a mountain, directing traffic to what we thought was some kind of winter sports resort or municipal campsite. And in the corner of this sign you could just make out in the dark and the rain a tiny stencil of a unicorn.

So we shot off in the car up this track, buoyed up with the knowledge that it did at least exist. The mountains were blanketed in evergreens and we could occasionally make out the sheer drops on the side of the road. There were no lights at all, no other cars, and absolutely no sign of human life. The road was potholed and muddy, and after another twelve slow kilometres I was beginning to have doubts that there was going to be anything at all at the end of the track.

Eventually, we saw some other cars, and then some people, and we knew we had got there at last. By this time it was about 1am; we parked the car and when we got out we could hear the music and see some lighting, although we still didn't know what to expect at all. It was hard to shake off the long journey and get into the mood to party and for a while I wasn't up for it at all. All I wanted to do was go to bed. And it was still raining, although (thank God) it wasn't cold.

Fortunately, we did have some pills on us. They're not very readily available in Japan, but if you know the right people (who are always foreign people: Iranians, Libyans, Brazilians and so on) you can get hold of them. And they're always the same out there: clear, gelatine capsules with 130mg of pure MDMA powder inside. Which is very nice indeed, and much better than anything you'd get in Britain, where many Es don't even contain MDMA and a good one will only have 60mg tops. And I had two of these capsules over the course of the night!

Back to the party; I took my first pill and we went down to the site. The old sign was right; it was a municipal campsite hired for the weekend by the organisers. You couldn't see much in the darkness but we could make out that there was a small river running through the middle of it with man-made concrete banks, a wood and rope suspension bridge over and a flat area on either side. There were some camper vans, tents, food stalls and shower blocks on one side, and the sound rig and lights on the other. Next to the rig was a huge tepee set up with a big campfire surrounded by people, along with flouro decorations and UV lights which were everywhere, contributing to the somewhat hippyish vibe.

There must have been about 500 people there all told; about half were Japanese and of the rest we were the only two English people. There were a lot of people we knew from Kyoto, all bang on; to drive that distance in those conditions you have to be fairly committed. We heard the next day that the organisers had expected up to 1000 people, but a lot of people must have thought *sod it* because of the rain. Most people had been there from much earlier in the day and about 100 or so drifted off during the course of the night when the rain didn't let up.

There was some good techno going on when we got there, but what I'll never forget about the music is that the area where people were dancing was two to three inches deep in really coarse gravel, so as well as the music and the rain you could hear this rhythmic *crunch, crunch, crunch* sound from everyone's feet as they were dancing. It was like a gravel percussion! So I started dancing to that, and as the night went on there was a couple of hours of deep, percussive house, New York style, which was also good. The DJ who came on after that played more trancey stuff which I didn't really like but by that stage I was so into it that I didn't really care; it's a beat, isn't it, and if you're partying madly and there's a beat you're going to jump up and down to it.

The very best moment for me, however, was when the light began to come up in the morning. We'd arrived at the site in the dark and rain, and I'd spent the night dancing in an area surrounded by almost pitch blackness, so I didn't know anything about what the place was like. But when the sun came up, it stopped raining, and I could see that we were near the summit of a hill, surrounded by more hills and mountains, on a plateau which was bisected by the river. And at the far end the hill rose up still further with a footpath going up with posts and rails, and as the dawn broke I decided to climb up.

I walked for about half a mile, to a point where I could look down on the whole site. And it was awesome. Low clouds were hanging around the tops of the tree-clad mountains, the dawn was breaking, the mist had settled in the valleys, and as far as the eye could see, there were miles and miles of mountains and forests, untamed and utterly beautiful. Looking down at the site I could see the little figures below me dancing and make out people chilling around the big fire in the middle of this vast wilderness . . .

Not long after this I went back to the car and fell asleep. We headed off at about half past ten, driving with a lot more caution now we could really see the sheer drops at the side of the narrow track. We were driving back to Tokyo, not Kyoto, and we estimated the drive would take about five hours, although it was in fact to take us eight.

Before we embarked on the journey, we decided to stop off at one of the hot springs which are quite common in that part of Japan. The set-up was in the grounds of a farmhouse, with a big hole dug into the ground roughly the size and shape of a large jacuzzi. It was perfect; we spent about one and a half hours just lying in this hot water, our heads back on the bank, having a smoke and chilling, contemplating the wooded valley below us and enjoying the view.

It was one of the first outdoor parties of that kind that Japan had ever seen, and from those beginnings a whole scene was to grow. The first big, organised, outdoor dance party, Rainbow 2000, took place in August 1995, with Underworld and CJ Bolland, amongst a lot of other well-known international dance acts. In 1996 Return To The Source did a big gig on the slopes of Mount Fuji, in 1997 the psychedelic trance scene really took off and now there are parties happening every weekend, with big-name DJs and proper, major publicity, organised by big commercial promoters. So you can see the way in which the outdoor party scene has taken off in Japan, going down much the same route, as far as organisation and promotion is concerned, that the rave scene did in the UK.

The difference is that so far, there has not been the same clash with the authorities that we saw over here; parties are organised well away from residential areas on the whole, the police and organisers work together more so there isn't the kind of confrontational 'them and us' scenario we take as the norm, and there isn't anything like the drug culture we have here. The Japanese girls we went to this party with were quite happy just drinking, and that seems to be the rule: they just don't do drugs like we do – not even smoking weed. And that's partly the reason why foreign DJs often really like playing in Japan, because people actually listen to what they're doing, without having their critical faculties blunted by being off their face. And although some parties have become very commercial, the underground party scene has been allowed to continue alongside because there hasn't been that clash with the authorities to drive it all above ground like we've seen here. Parties like the one I went to are still going on in Japan, four years later, as well as the huge industry which has grown from those early days.

Jake

Entering the Brewery Tap, one of the many pubs that satellite the Young's Brewery in Wandsworth, the crowd we were about to join were discernible from the locals in both age and attire. The brownish, reddish hues of pub culture added to the anticipation of the night ahead. This was only a meeting place: we were about to enter a world far removed from thickly patterned carpets and picture-postcards of horses and drays. It was the opening night of London's legendary Club UK.

We turned into a dark side-street off the main road. Already a large crowd were forming a rough queue to the right of the venue – a large, windowless warehouse – a row of bouncers marking the two entrance gates. High above us spotlights illuminated a large steel sign with the words 'Club UK' cut out of it. One of our crowd, Matt, ushered us into the left-hand door and up to a girl with a clipboard marking our names off the sacred guest list.

A dark corridor took us into the room we had heard most about: the Pop-Art Room. With its Warhol stacks of giant wooden Brillo and Campbell's Soup boxes, this was like no other club. The factory atmosphere altered as we entered the Smart Bar. Here 'smart' drinks were being bought before approaching a more serious dance situation than the Pop Art room.

Already the floor was solid with dancers facing the illuminated DJ booth which seemed to lurch on to the dancefloor itself. The crowd pulsed to the thumping sound system, sweating and clutching bottles of water. The DJ seemed to throw energy out to the adoring crowd as they waved in appreciation of a hip break. Light beams illuminated the naked torsos dancing on huge speaker stacks.

Matt pulled his record box into the booth. We levered ourselves onto the dance floor. He began his set with a seamless crossover from the track playing. The crowd rose up in delight.

Dom, London

Helter Skelter, Oxford: Helter Skelter was a huge event; it cost £25, and when you think that everything prior to it had been free or a maximum of £15, that was a lot of money. But the line-up was amazing, so we got our tickets and went, and for once everyone who was supposed to be there was there. The KLF were playing, not on stage, but on a bloody great tower which until that point had been used to bounce the lasers off. We could see them, a couple of guys hanging off this tower with keyboards around their necks. I was out of it: I'd had a couple of Es already, and by this point I'd done a trip as well, and I remember thinking this was pretty outrageous. And it was to get more so: suddenly, in the middle of their act, all this paper started fluttering down on to the crowd. We all thought it must be monopoly money, but I caught a bit and realised it was a Scottish pound note. I couldn't really focus that well, but I could just about make out that on the back of it they had written Children, we love you. *So I'm catching this stuff as it's coming down, and I ended up with a whole bunch of it, and I thought I was rich.* It's not real money, *says this bloke to me.* Yes it is; it's Scottish money, mate, *I said.* You mean this is real money? *he yells. And before you know it everyone's scrambling around for it, on their hands and knees, the money still floating down in the dark, and it seemed like madness, like anarchy, and it was the best feeling.*

Simon, London

It was at Boy George's birthday party and the opening night of Amnesia in Ibiza back in '88. Everyone who was anyone converged on the island that week for a massive party. The acid house thing had just begun to explode; although it still retained a strong underground vibe where everyone knew everyone. The clubs which belong in House music folklore had now become well established: Clink Street, Enter the Dragon, The Trip, Sin, Shoom, Future and Confusion.

I went with a group of friends and DJs who were on the circuit at that time. We flew out to Ibiza and rented a villa in the mountains and when it came to the night of the party we got there and saw that there were about two thousand people there, everyone totally on one. There were half-naked people dancing in the fountains, people walking around the massive outdoor site with watering-cans full of crushed Es, pouring it into people's drinks; you wouldn't believe it. Everyone was on the same buzz; it was the perfect party. There were all sorts, from trannies, gays, terrace trendies (football firms), so many different types of people. You could never recapture it. It was the original vibe which exploded into the Summer of Love when all the people who were there brought it back to this country and brought with them what we now call the Balearic sound.

One DJ I was with out there, Nicky H., had never done acid before and he decided whilst we were out there to do a trip. He did it towards the end of the night because we could doss by the pool all day. When we came out he was just beginning to feel the effects. We had a hire car and we were just leaving when we ran into Dave, a famous photographer, who was wandering around looking for his friend. So we offered him a lift and he got in, not knowing what condition Nicky was in – he seemed all right at the time and hadn't started tripping out or anything yet. So we drove off, and suddenly realised that we'd forgotten where we were staying! We knew it was in the mountains, though, so we headed for the hills and started driving around looking for the villa.

We got to the top of the mountain on this little winding road and suddenly Nicky, who was driving, started freaking out on the acid and totally forgot that he was driving a car. He let go of the steering-wheel and hung out of the side window of the car waving both hands in the air and then started trying to jump out of the window! Dave, who was sitting in the back, thought we were all going to die and started screaming, *Stop the car! Stop the car!*

Eventually, we got Nicky to stop the car and Dave got out and sat at the side of the road shaking – this was in the mountains, in the middle of nowhere – and refused to get back in. You should have seen his face! When we did persuade him, and when Nicky had calmed down a bit as well, we had to drive away at about ten miles per hour. We still didn't know where the villa was, but when we found it eventually, Dave had to have a strong black coffee and sit down for an hour . . . and to this day he's never got back in a car with Nicky H.

Dillon, London

We went to Love Muscle at The Fridge that night in celebration of something or other. It is often the case these days that one does not require a specific purpose. Everyone knows that as the night takes its course, there will be moments when the whole concept of life itself will seem reason enough. Through the course of the evening one will reach great levels of intimacy with friends and strangers alike and perhaps, with oneself. At times it may seem that one is skirting on the parameters of the greatest joys and the greatest sorrows of one's life simultaneously, viewing them all with a reassuring acceptance coupled with a stimulating reverie.

It must have been about four o'clock in the morning when we heard the news of the death of Princess Diana, a loving spirit and perhaps the nation's most famous carer. It shook everyone in the way that hard reality always does when one was previously at one's most euphoric. I personally realised for the first time in that moment what she had symbolised for so many people. It was as though the old had lost a daughter and the young a mother. People felt a personal connection with Diana. She had a great talent for accessibility on an almost inconceivable scale.

For the remainder of that night we danced in celebration of life, and of having shared a lifetime with one who somehow managed to inspire so much love not only throughout a nation, but across the world. As we threw our hands into the air, it was as though to build a ladder of spirit that, having been released from the body, a soul might climb unhindered and with ease to its next destination.

Maz, Herne Hill

Norwich Energy, 23 September 1989: We hit the road at the usual time, in a convoy of cars, stopping at service stations to phone for the next set of directions. There were thousands of cars, and I mean thousands, on the road, all heading for this do, and I remember we got to some small town and found there was a road-block. It was a B road, and nothing was moving. The cars going to the rave were on both sides of the road; if anything had wanted to come the other way, it couldn't have done. We were somewhere near the front. I got out of the car to see what was going on and wandered up to the road-block. The police were telling everyone that the event wasn't where we had been told, it was in a totally different direction. Although we were suspicious, they said they had no reason to lie to us, and that the event wasn't this way, it was three miles back the other way. They gave us specific directions, and as soon as these began to filter back to the people in the cars, I remember watching what looked like thousands of cars trying to turn around in the B road and go back the way they had come. It was mayhem!

We did eventually find the site, which turned out to be a relatively small aircraft hangar on Ministry of Defence land. We parked up, and got into a queue of people, watched closely by security. In those days, the security wasn't official, it was villains with pit bulls and bloody great torches more often than not. Really heavy, keeping everyone in line . . . I was one of the first people in the hangar and you could see that there had been no preparation for the event – there was machinery and tools, expensive equipment all over the place, most of which was gone by the morning! By which time the security had completely lost control of the event, there were so many people. They gave up at about eight and turned it into a free party. Eventually, the sound system outside on the truck was linked up to the one in the hangar so half the party was outside, which was just as well because you weren't going to get over six thousand people in the hangar.

It was a daytime do, and there was all sorts of madness going on. What I remember most was about one in the afternoon, Jarvis (who used to run all the Biology events) came on the mike. He stopped the music, and asked if anyone had a mobile phone, because there were some cars on fire outside. People were hiding their phones, because they were too out of it to call, and besides, half of us didn't know where our phones were anyway. He went on to say that if you had parked your car to the right-hand side of the stage, you should go and check if it was yours on fire. Eventually, I wandered out to see what was happening and there were four cars on fire – not just the engines, but flames coming out of every part of them. There were three or four hundred people standing around by the time I got out, watching in a semicircle, and one car doing handbrake turns through the blazing cars. Most of the cars were hire cars, so no one was that bothered. One of our friends, Nick, who was really out of it, was warming his hands on one! Then he started freaking everyone out, saying that his friend was asleep in the car, and that it was his car. People thought he was really cool when they saw him dancing later, despite the loss of car, friend and possessions. He didn't have the heart to tell them he had been winding them up.

I found out later how the do ended at the hangar. It had originally been organised for a different site, but the police found out about it and stopped it going ahead. So the organisers kept the convoys of cars on the road all night, thousands of them, directing them from place to place, whilst they frantically tried to find another site. The place we all ended up at had already been considered previously, but had been turned down on the grounds that it was Ministry of Defence property and too risky. But that's where we ended up, and the whole thing came off and it turned out to be a brilliant event. It was totally anarchic; there was no order there, except that everyone was there to have a good time. And it was that which bound people together and ensured there was so little trouble or violence. We all looked after each other and what trouble there was usually came from the police.

Simon, London

The first Sunrise party was a landmark. Driving towards it you could see nothing in front of you but a river of red tail-lights and nothing behind you but a river of white headlights, stretching as far as the eye can see. And there's people hanging out of the sunroofs and out of the windows, and as you get closer to the site you begin to hear the music and you can see the lasers in the sky and the big wheel at the site getting closer . . . and we danced all night and watched the dawn come up in the morning, still dancing . . .

Ralf E. P. (Oracle), Birmingham

brief encounters

I've met some really cool people when I've been out clubbing.
We've all had that kind of conversation with a stranger that goes
on for what seems like hours, that at the end of you find yourself
convinced that they are your soulmate, your best friend, the only
person who really and truly shares your experience. This often
happens in the toilet; after a while you become wary and only go
when it's absolutely necessary, because you can quite easily spend
a whole night in there debating the importance of run-proof
mascara to modern clubbing, or the ascendancy of Nike over
Adidas, or whether Britain is still Great, or whether the Spice Girls
ever made a contribution to late-twentieth-century feminism. But
for some people that's what it's all about, and they're quite happy
spending a night in the can; for me, I'm there to dance and that's
it. Talking's for the next day, when I'm coming down with my
friends at home. So I'm wary of the toilets. It's partly a speed thing;
whatever you're doing at that moment is the best thing in the world
to be doing and it's very hard to drag yourself away. So you get
stuck on the dancefloor for hours, and you can equally get stuck
in the toilet for hours. And then you get stuck to your sofa the next
day when you're coming down, even though there's crap on the
TV and the remote control is just out of reach, and you really want
to get up, and you will, any moment . . .

But like I said, I've met some real characters. I was at the first
night of Absolute at the Coliseum in Vauxhall, a sadly short-lived
night, and there was this old guy really giving it some on the
dance platform. He had a Hawaiian shirt on, and a tie, and a
trilby would you believe it. He was well up for it, and everyone
was loving it, seeing him going for it. He wasn't short of water or

people to talk to all night. I eventually went over and said hello, and it turned out he was seventy-three, and had followed the DJ all over Europe, dancing like a maniac every time he played.

And there used to be one guy who you'd often see at Voyager at The Complex in Islington. He was in a wheelchair, but he must have burned off as much energy as anyone else in there. He always looked totally focused, totally concentrated on the music, and so I never went to talk to him. He was in his own world. I haven't seen him for ages; I don't know if he still goes clubbing somewhere else or gave it up.

There are always faces you see time and time again, and sometimes you get to know them and they become friends, and sometimes there's mutual recognition of each other as regulars and you smile at each other but never introduce yourself and sometimes they just remain part of what makes the club for you – you see them, and know you're really here and it's going to be a good night. I've sometimes wondered how it would feel to see them out of context, on the train for example, or in Burger King. Would you recognise them at all?

And last weekend someone came up to me and said, *I see you here every Friday night and you're always really going for it . . .* So I found myself one of the ones who other people always see, part of the club, part of the night for someone else. And I like that, but it's strange as well; a slight loss of identity that's both odd and strangely intoxicating.

Anon

That's it. Max decides he must be in hell. He tries to shut his brain off, he wants to go to sleep, he wants to die. This trip has turned into a white-knuckle, roller-coaster ride which he went on unwittingly for a thrill but it is so wildly intense that he's totally shit-scared. The only consolation is that it can't last for ever. He hopes.

Max has long since stopped consciously listening to the music in the club. His brain has turned down the impact of its volume. It has become a distant throb, a pulsing boom. Where are all his friends? If Max could manage it, he'd wander around the club and find them.

Everything resembles a painting by Hieronymus Bosch; a writhing and twisted purgatory of pain. Perpetual waves of extreme paranoia and discomfort slosh over him, unrelentlessly slashing his nervous system.

Max senses someone sit next him. *All right?* a sharp female voice asks.

His eyes focus but assume she's a hallucination. Boggle-eyed, he slowly stretches out a finger to discover whether she's real. Yep, it's her. Of all the times and places to meet again the blonde raver of his dreams from Helter Skelter, this has got to be the very worst. Not only is he totally off his nut, he feels extremely ugly too. He strains to swallow, but can't. *How's it goin'?* she smiles.

Max tries to gabble something back but his brain and mouth fail him. She's so beautiful, an aura of golden light appears to shine around her like the old Ready Brek adverts. Waves of awe and topsy-turvy drugs swirl through his system. He is not in control. *Are you all right?* The girl's rounded forehead is creased with concern. The strange idea that she might care something about him minutely makes up for the fact that he's too twatted to communicate. *Yeah . . . Sorry, I . . . I feel weird,* he mutters. *You rushin'?* she asks. *Kind of . . . it's . . . a . . . a . . . acid.* A juicy laugh ripples out of her marvellous mouth before she can stop herself. *Aw, sorry mate. I'm really sorry. It's just that now you've mentioned it, I can see it. Freaky, isn't it?* Max nods meekly, a disturbing mix of emotions flooding over him. He's angry and embarrassed at being so helpless and possibly fucking up his only chance with her, and somewhere deep, deep inside, good old-fashioned lust rears its ugly head.

An extended silence stretches out between the pair. Max is desperate to say something, pull her closer and show her that he cares. Her spry little thighs thump up and down to the beat of the music and her chewing intensifies. Instant paranoia that she's bored and about to go causes him to frantically try and rise above the drug and say something interesting, something devastating. *Isn't that tree . . . isn't it, isn't it just . . .* he manages. *Yeah, it's nice* she says.

He regrets mentioning the tree immediately. She's smiling but he's too confused to effectively work out whether she's really bored or taking the piss. The two of them are on different drugs, different vibes. Max feels fucked up, wasted – a total mess. She stands up to go, her body literally shaking as the effort to sit still becomes too much. *I'm going to dance. Oh . . .* Max croaks defeatedly, painfully lonely already. Demurely she gazes down at him. *What's your name?* Max raises his head, surprised and pleased that she's bothered to ask. *Max* he croaks. *Mine's Ross. Well, see you around Max – have a nice trip.* She winks and turns to leave, swallowed back into the crowd. As he watches her go he feels momentarily better. Then in a wave the dizzy drug returns, clamping on to his skull like a crushing heavyweight of metal.

Daniel Newman, London

Anton the Pirate was a real character everyone used to know back in '88 and '89. He was always around; worked for a lot of people. He had big long dreadlocks, must have been two or three feet long. That was his calling card; he was everywhere, a proper party man.

Anyway, Sunrise put on an event in Slough at an equestrian centre. It was pissing down with rain and everyone had been driving around to find it for hours and man, it stank of horses in there. They had these massive industrial heaters in there to try and dry the place out, and Anton the Pirate comes in soaking wet from the rain, notices the heaters and thinks to himself, Great, I'll go and dry my hair! *So he's stuck his head in front of one of these huge heaters, stood there for a bit and all of a sudden his hair's melted! All the dreadlocks melted into one huge lump and he hadn't noticed the smell because it already stank enough in there.*

Dillon, London

Nothing bores me more than those pumpkin lanterns, skeleton masks and the whole ensemble of tack and nonsense that accompanies Hallowe'en. You're having a laugh if you think for one minute I'd partake. I'd prefer to do nothing, and remain fully honourable. Well, that was the plan.

Late as usual, I doubted that they'd even be there, an hour is usually on the threshold of people's waiting time. Pubs generally keep most people occupied though, and by the time I arrived you could say my friends were occupied, not incredibly coherent, but occupied nonetheless; they even pooh-poohed my tardiness as the norm. This leads me to a plethora of questions:

1. Why is it that whenever I turn up to the pub late I always end up drinking more than anyone else?

2. Why is it that I always seem to end up encouraging outrageous behaviour in such situations?

3. Why do I always spend more money than everyone else?

4. Why does my drunken oblivion generally enter the world of sex? Is it:

a. I have an inferiority complex?

b. I am an animal?

c. I am a mug?

d. I am a sexual deviant?

I tell you, if you could answer those questions, I'd be one sorted motherfucka.

So back to October 31st, drunkenness took its usual route and a place for further frivolity was the general consensus – well, necessity. Luckily, one of my friends was mobile and we all piled into his Range Rover – oh, to have loaded parents. We arrived back at my place swiftly and decided that it would be a jolly good idea to get out all of Alistaire's dresses he ripped off from Hobbs. They were jolly, frilly and, after all, it was Hallowe'en.

Dressed up to the nines, legs out and make-up glittering, we all piled into the car – back in the pub five minutes later we caused a general stir and decided the best plan was to get the hell out of there. In retrospect, it was a very clever move. Three hours later, dribbling by now, we had reached our destination, a muddy field in deepest Norfolk; we'd have never got there if it wasn't for the phat bass which must have guided us the last ten miles. We spewed out of the car, and in that state of slightly dizzy expectation grooved through the gate and into the first tent. Places like that always freak me out, having to piss in bushes, only having strong lager to drink, or if you're lucky and get there early enough you have the honour of supping water from a huge vat that cows have probably been using earlier that afternoon. Luck wasn't on my side and I was confronted with a particularly unsettling sight. I don't know if you've met any heavy strong-lager drinkers, but their vomit tends to be orange and glutinous. This be-dreadlocked scumsucker was no different; the puke formed a layer not unsimilar to a great oil leak, but probably infinitely more toxic. Back to the tent . . .

Mouth as dry as a pie of old bones, I started fantasising about wetness – wetness of any sort. My eyes scanned the room looking for satiation, and I found it in the nubile girl wiggling in front of me. Those moist lips were positively oozing cool liquid.

I became the lolly she was avidly sucking, swilled around by that cool moist tongue. The darkness didn't bother me, I just needed to be in her mouth – oh bastion of pleasure. I need to be in there, my conscious was telling me, not all this fantasising tosh; she was smiling at me after all.

Unsteadily, I rose to my feet and involuntarily lurched in her direction: shocked, she backed away and gave me a very quizzical look. I gurned back in the most alluring way I could manage, and laughingly she took the two steps forward that she had manoeuvred back. I was obviously harmless. By this time, I had recovered my motion and started swaying to the juicy beat. Oh yeah, this is what it's all about. I swaggered next to her, feeling the warmth of her body captured very enticingly in a pure black catsuit complete with tail and ears. This is what Heaven feels like. Surely? Hands making circular movements around her delicate frame I was there, she belonged to me – me, me, me, me. Ha, who needs water when you have wine?

Dancing like that for hours, my lips touched her perfumed neck. I breathed in, sucking in as much air as my lungs allowed. I staggered, the ground rose and swallowed me, the cold damp grass was beneath me. I looked up and saw her in the arms of another man – what the hell's goin' on? The philanderer, adulterer, hell-bitch from planet Fuck. A hand reached down, it was the scab who'd stolen her. *Meet Mark, my boyfriend* she said through gnashing teeth. I took his hand and whilst murmuring a reply I darted off to find the next piece of wet grass, which incidentally was just in front of me. Face down, I sucked in the moisture, which had probably been stamped on many times already that evening. It didn't bother me; after all, what good could I have been to her in that state anyway? Besides, my fantasy was still lingering, face down on the ground, sure, but if the truth be known, I was still there, swaying to the beat of her thighs. Boyfriend? *Pah.*

I must have remained in this state of confused abandon for some time, as when I clicked out of it she was gone, and so was everyone else by the looks of things. Just those few, always left at the end, talking or muttering to themselves like they always do. Looking up through crossed eyes, I couldn't help but notice the crusty from before still vomiting. Following the blast of vomit, I traced it back to the lake of moisture I had just raised my head from. Oh Lord. Replacing my head in the quagmire, I turned my palms to the sky and prayed to God for the first time in my life. *Is this what it's all about?* I pleaded.

Yes, came my psyche's jubilant response. It had finally happened, I was in hell. Still, I suppose it could have been worse. The drugs could have been shit.

No sooner had I discovered my stark awakening than I heard a shout from somewhere, *Ants, where the hell you been man?*

Where are you? I muttered. *Here man, you fuck-up*, the voice said. *Come on, we're going back; the pub opens in an hour . . .*

And it did.
Anton Garby, Brixton

I've been taking Es for years, so not much surprises me any more. But fifteen minutes after taking this one I felt this amazing rush, as if I was tingling all over. I had never felt so great on an E. And that's when it happened. I looked across the chill-out room and my eyes locked on to the eyes of this gorgeous guy. He looked in his early twenties and he wore one white glove. He smiled. I smiled. It all happened in slow motion. We started to walk towards each another, stepping over the people sitting and lying on the floor and met in the middle of the room. I was feeling all wobbly as he took hold of my hands, sat me down and told me I had a fantastic smile. He told me he'd had a Shamrock and that his name was Tony and we spent the rest of the night talking, dancing and kissing.

We spent the next two years together as partners and now we are best friends. It was the best night of my life.

I still go raving, but only once a month now and although I've just turned forty, I still enjoy the atmosphere and love meeting new people. My eighteen-year-old daughter comes with me and we both agree you can't beat a night out at Cream.
Lynne, Chester

I've made more close friends when I've been out clubbing than I did at school, or college, or at work. If you go out with a smile on your face and a positive attitude you can't help it. Partly it's getting a load of like-minded people in a room together; they're bound to make friends with each other. And partly it's the music, which whether it's uplifting and positive or concentrated and focusing, channels people's energies in a single direction – dancing – rather than people getting bored and looking for a fight or trying to pull.

But mostly it's the drugs. When was the last time you saw a load of pissed-up blokes smiling and hugging and dancing together, telling each other how much they valued each other, exchanging phone numbers and looking out for each other? Alcohol is a destructive drug. It is addictive and anti-social, leads to violence and drink-driving, and all kinds of alcohol-related diseases. When we hear our parents' generation moralising about ecstasy, why should we listen when we see them poisoning themselves and condoning something so destructive and anti-social, something that has nothing to redeem it all?

It *is* easier to make friends when you are on an E. But the friendships themselves are not any the less for having been made on E and can be just as lasting. It's just that the barrier of distrust and reserve is removed so you can be open and trusting with other people. That is why clubbing can be such an empowering experience: you go out and lay yourself wide open to people in a way you can't do in your normal life, and nothing bad comes of it. Your trust is not abused and you take that away with you. So you benefit even when you are *not* on E just from knowing that such an experience is possible, and you go about trying to bring it into your day-to-day life and your dealings with people. I know so many people who are more together and much happier for having done a pill; I know this sounds evangelical, but I and most people I know have found it to be true.

I am not talking about E *abuse,* but E *use,* which means responsible and sensible use, not excessive or over-use. Often, the people who misuse ecstasy are the people who used to be beer monsters and have been converted to ecstasy. They bring the same 'down-the-hatch' machismo bravado philosophy to their drug use, which can make it just as destructive, to themselves if not to other people.

One of the best things about clubbing is that you meet people and make friends in a way you never do when you go out drinking in pubs. Dance music and the ecstasy culture have brought together different types of people who otherwise may not have met, and it has produced a very positive, caring, responsible culture, contrary to how the mainstream media portray it. This is the truth behind the headlines, which every serious clubber reading this will recognise. We have built something very strong and very important and very positive for ourselves, so let's make sure we keep it that way.
Paul Belford, Isle of Wight

It had been a funny old Glastonbury from the word Go. The first problem was, well . . . *cherchez la femme.* I'd recently been dumped by my girlfriend, who we'll call Emma. Emma was the most amazing woman I'd ever met and I wasn't dealing with the break-up very well at all. She was still one of the gang, though, so I'd come to Glastonbury knowing she'd be there. I was nervous about seeing her, but I was determined to try not to let that stop me having a good time.

Problem number two was, there was another couple in our group who'd recently split, and what with them not wanting to camp together and me and Emma not wanting to camp together, we were split up into little factions, and I was camped up near the movie field with the other recently split-up girl and her new boyfriend. Now, camping with a new couple probably wasn't that fantastic an idea, because they spent a lot of time in their tent, so I spent a fair bit of time on my own, and wandering around Glastonbury on your own takes a certain amount of . . . I don't know what of, exactly, maybe confidence, swagger, self-assuredness? Things I wasn't too full of at the time.

And then there was the drugs issue. I'd come prepared: there was a little snap bag in my pocket with a quarter of hash, a couple of Es, a wrap and a couple of trips – you know, your typical Glastonbury-style 'something for the weekend'. Sorted, as they say. Anyway, Friday night I was wandering around on my own, speeding my tits off, and at about four in the morning I found myself at a little café-style stall down in Babylon, surrounded by people dancing to some quite nice melodic trance. *This is all right*, I thought, *I'll just sit here and have a little smoke and people-watch*. So I sat down, got out my little bag and started putting a spliff together, when suddenly four homeboys appeared out of nowhere. One of them grabbed the bag – *What's this? Any Es in there mate? Got any trips?* I reached out to grab it back and was pushed back in my seat by two of the others; then they just walked off, taking my little stash with them.

Waah! Problem number three.

So Saturday came, and found me wandering around still on my own, still heartbroken, and now unwillingly drug-free. The latter kind of managed to sort itself out – I didn't have the cash to replace all that I'd lost, but I did bump into a few people I knew, one of whom sold us an E and one of whom gave us a bit of hash on borrowsies. Then, sat up by the stone circle mid-afternoon I'd bought a trip off a passing hippy, had a little nibble, then bumped into a mate and we'd necked the rest. It was good acid and we had a fine old evening, just wandering around laughing at things, feeling nice and trippy without losing the plot to too great a degree. But by midnight, my mate was happily sitting round a fire sharing a pipe, whereas I had a Saturday-night head on and was in need of a groove.

So I went looking for a groove.

At this point, things looked like looking up. I was intending to find the rest of the people I'd come with; instead, as I got to the gate between the NME and circus fields (I think it was), I met a whole bunch of lads we knew from Manchester. They'd just arrived and were carting all their stuff in – including beers which they were flogging for a quid a can. So they gave us a couple of cans and we arranged to meet at the jazz tent at 1.30, when Zion Train were on.

This was more like it! Hey, I might be unloveable and skint, but at least I can still wander around Glastonbury and meet up with mates and get free beer. Think I'll have that E then . . .

So I sat by another café with music, had a couple of coffees and watched the world go by until it was time to go to the jazz tent. And then it all started going wrong again: I couldn't find the others. I looked everywhere, but no sign. The only people I could see that I recognised were the guys that had mugged us the night before, who were hanging around the fringes of the tent looking threatening (or at least, so it seemed to me. Looking back I suppose it might not have been them at all, but I was convinced at the time). By now the E was really kicking in, only the music was a bit too smoky and dubby to really throw yourself around to: I kept trying, then having a bit of a sit down because my head was going mad, then trying to dance again. At one point, I sat down and had a spliff, then tried to dance once more, but again it wasn't really happening, so I decided I'd have another spliff . . .

Only of course I'd left it where I was sat before, and it wasn't there any more. Stupid bastard! By now I was really pissed off. This was the second lot of hash I'd lost in two days; there were people who'd mugged me all over the place, no sign of my friends . . . headspin! Headspin! Right, get a grip: the only reason my head was fucked up, I decided, was that I was full of energy with no outlet for it, so why not go for a nice pacey stomp around the field, work it off, maybe bump into someone I knew . . . which is what I did.

And it was at the gate into the next field that I had one of the strangest encounters of my life. I was just walking along, looking around me, when a voice said: *It's mad, innit?* I turned around and there was this crusty, traveller type walking by my side. *You what, mate?* I asked. *I said, it's mad, innit? You come here, to a festival, and there's all the lights and the people and the music, and you're on a mind-altering drug that you've tried to expand your consciousness with, so you're using parts of your brain you don't use normally, and it's just all mad, it's a bit much, innnit?*

Now this I could deal with. Poor lad was obviously a bit overwhelmed. I'm good at sorting people's heads out, I could cope with this. So I put my arm around the guy and said *Aah, you're a man after my own heart. Yeah, you're right, it's mad, innit?* And we sort of bear-hugged, and then I asked him his name. *Ah. Some people call me one thing,* he said, stepping forward and turning around so he was walking backwards in front of me, *and some people call me another. My parents gave me one name,* and here he paused, and held one finger up, as we both stood still and looked at each other, *and who am I to disagree?*

And then he disappeared.

I mean it, I swear. He just disappeared. He didn't turn around and walk off, or anything like that, he just disappeared – in a puff of smoke, only without the smoke. Bizarre.

Anyway, I've thought a lot about this since. Maybe the guy was some sort of guardian angel; maybe I was just more off my head than I thought. At the time I got annoyed because, hey, I could handle my drugs, and who was some smart-arse pseudo-mystical crusty to tell me I couldn't? But then with that thought came one of those I'm-all-right-now moments of clarity: yes, I could handle my drugs, what was the problem? Get back to the tent and have a good time you mawky bastard! Which I did, and the rest of the night was pretty much fine.

So I guess what I'm really trying to say is, whoever or whatever you were, Mr Incredible Disappearing Man – cheers mate!
Russ Leonardson, Bath

foreign parts

Being a Belgian bloke it wasn't easy to get to Köln for the Mayday event, nor to find the venue where the rave of all raves takes place. Around midnight, I park my car amongst thousands of others. My Belgian number plate fits nicely among the German, French, Swedish and Italian.

Next to mine three Germans step out of their car. They open the boot of the car, dress up like maintenance people in a nuclear plant, put on gas masks and head for the entrance of the arena.

The massive gates reveal a *Blade Runner* world crowded with sweaty bodies driven by a pounding beat generated by a machine developed in California to study earthquakes. In the middle of a dancefloor the size of a football pitch, a gigantic black box barfs up basswaves that make your teeth gnash to the rhythm of the beat. A giant wave of ten thousand bodies united under one laser flash submerges the vast dancefloor. The energy generated by the crowd explodes in my mind. It's like a thousand bees eating their way through my brain and bouncing up and down under my skull.

My girlfriend to my left and best friend to my right start dancing as if they have no option – and they don't. The light-effects and laser beams explode above our heads and flow over our shoulders and bodies.

We blend in and learn the meaning of peace, unity, love. These words are no longer a symbol man uses to pinpoint a certain feeling. These words are now vivid, full of reason.

foreign parts

I no longer exist as a unit. The entity called Gery is split up. My body is in a trance and keeps on repeating the same movements. My mind has lost control. I surf on the vibes, my skull is crushed and my mind becomes free. I become part of the pure energy, I *am* pure energy. I see the crowd black and shapeless, yet friendly and warm. Here and there I see white dots: the power plant outfitters. Time is no longer an issue. It stops. The beat is like a clock ticking the same second over and over again. We beat the clock, together as one.

When I come to my senses I appear to have lost my friends in the whirling mass. Somebody nearby blows a horn (some brought whistles, why not a horn?). As in a fairy-tale, in the blur a gate consisting of two naked bodies opens and out pops my girlfriend and friend. Still in a trance. Empty faces screwed on to bodies which have lost all sense of direction. Their eyes are like cheap marbles inserted into big black holes.

As the music is stopped for a change of DJs we head for the bar. I bounce on to a bundle of muscles. He spills his beer all over his pants. He turns around and . . . excuses himself for being in my way. Peace, love.

Later that night we meet Heidi, a Switzerland-based raver, and a funny, five-foot-tall Japanese Adidas training-suit with a couple of big eyes on it. He asks if all European discos are like this. We confirm that each weekend it's like this. He talks about moving to Europe.

Four am: our muscles are getting tired. Our heads want more, more of that feeling of being freed from the body, becoming one with sound. Captagon clears our head and Vicks (the menthol cream) covers our heads and shoulders. We smell like hell but feel like an Eskimo skating on ice. Like African tribes, we dance around the fire and are haunted by friendly spirits who take us up to a higher level of consciousness. Man is one tribe. The fire is techno. The DJ is the shaman. Techno is music for your belly. That's why so many are afraid of it: it takes over your reason. It takes control of your thoughts. It expands your mind. Ultimately, it's a drug.

Ten a.m.: some trance experiences later we head for the car, knowing that we are one. The sun is shining and people lie down all over the lawns surrounding the stadium. Everybody is talking to everybody. Speaking another language is no problem to understanding each other. This is unity. This is love.
Gery & Wendy, Belgium

Space, the Final Frontier: Space Closing Party, Ibiza, September 1997: It's funny, over ten years have passed since I started rejecting the suits and shazzas at the local Cinderella Rockafella. Earliest memories of my immersion into dance music are listening to Pete Tong on Capital Radio on Saturday nights and my hooded-topped-self standing outside a disused warehouse in High Wycombe with a bottle of wine instead of a sneaky trip.

Those early days followed a pattern that was repeated up and down the country: hook up with your mates, go to a motorway service station (Hendon was always my favourite), have a blinder at a rave and roll back home at an unearthly hour. I left High Wycombe in 1990 to study a business studies course in Southampton, which I left as soon as I could after realising what a desert it was.

Next stop was Nottingham. This was more like it! Women, bars, infamous clubs like Venus, Kool Kat, the Dance Factory and the DIY collective. I ended the first half of my clubland decade in one of the best cities in the country, inspired by pirate radio stations like Rave FM and DJs from across the country flocking to this East Midlands Mecca.

However, I had to move back to London in autumn 1992 to study. This second part of the decade has produced some mesmerising memories for me: meeting friends who are with me to this day (and not the fickle kind of folk that you can meet in clubs), seeing Lil' Louie Vega and Kenny Dope Gonzalez four-deck mixing in the Ministry, Glastonbury, Gay Pride, Summer Rites, Notting Hill Carnivals, New Year's Eve in Amsterdam, Billion Dollar Babes, Fierce Child, Love Ranch, come-down parties at my flat, going to work with no sleep, talking about how we were going to change the world, Sound Factory Bar in New York, and of course Ibiza.

I'd really thought I'd seen it all until I went to the best party ever in September 1997. After years of hearing how superb/shite Ibiza was, I decided to get my arse into gear and go over to *the* Balearic island. I'd already been 'larging it' (as Monsieur Tong would say) for a week, but I knew the closing party for Space on Sunday would be the big one. Posters were tantalisingly draped around Ibiza challenging you not to attend.

Saturday evening finally arrived and instead of burning ourselves out we had a couple of drinks and an early night, getting to bed by three am. We got down to Space at eleven am next morning and after queuing for half an hour in the multilingual heave, my friend James and I got in and headed straight for the terrace bar. What makes Space special is that it is split into two areas. The first area is a normal indoors club while the second area is a terrace, and it was here that I was to spend the next twelve years of my life. It was a huge area, surrounded by palm trees and covered by camouflaging netting and drapes. It was beautifully colour co-ordinated with vivid blues, purples and oranges mixing with clouds and angels that hung from the roof to create the impression of rising above the earth and literally up to space.

The terrace was fairly empty so we wandered inside to take a peek. The sight of the crowded dancefloor was absolutely amazing. The music being played was a mixture of warped disco and tech house that was weaving its magic on the audience. Performers were shaking their moneymakers on the stage when a white sheet descended on to the crowd until it covered the whole dancefloor. Two huge sparklers on the roof erupted into life covering the sheet with incendiary sparks while a neon sign burst into life with the words 'see you next year'. It makes my head buzz even now because I can still see the huge grins as the crowd pushed the sheet up and down to that all-time classic house tune – Jaydee, 'Plastic Dreams'. The sparklers continued raining down on to the crowd for ten minutes, supercharging the crowd for the long day ahead. After this amazing start we wandered outside into the thirty-degree heat to continue dancing.

By the early afternoon, the terrace was awash with people and I realised why this party was so good. It was the perfect combination of different nationalities, drugs, drink, straights, gays, freaks, UK lager-louts, trannies, music and hedonistic attitudes. The music outside was more garage moving into speedy garage and modern disco in a seamless mix by Alfredo and Alex Klein. I can remember saying to James, *It doesn't get much better than this,* and he agreed.

The only downer was the fact that a drink cost £5 a pop! After spending £25 to get in I hardly had any money so, much to my shame, I resorted to trying to nick other people's drinks. However I got caught red-handed by the owner of a delicious-looking vodka, so I had to put that idea on the backburner. By seven pm I could go no further without a drink so I had a much-needed time out and went to the local shops. I got a two-litre bottle of San Miguel, a bottle of water and a bottle of orange juice (gotta get those vitamins!). It was a sight to behold when I came out of that shop. Playa d'en Bossa (where Space is) is a family resort and it was a bizarre sight to see old people and families looking completely shocked by groups of people wandering around smashed.

After an hour of talking nonsense to some guy from Northampton, we decided to head back to the club. As we approached, the opening keys of 'Around the World' by Daft Punk burst from the terrace. I started running and James followed in hot pursuit. Unfortunately for him, he tripped over a bit of wire and did the sort of really painful flyer that you used to do at school. Poor sod got quite badly cut up, as he grazed his arm and stomach and was bleeding from the cuts. We patched him up inside and got back to the dancefloor. By nine pm the floor was in full sway with people dancing, waving, hollering and generally losing it. Although I was starting to feel tired, the music and atmosphere would not let me go. I vaguely remember saying goodbye to James because he had to get the plane back that night whereas I was staying in Ibiza for another week. I shuffled my way around the club and hooked up with my flatmate Kate, who was also there. The next couple of hours were spent dancing with various people and getting a buzz off the fact that you could dance with complete strangers and they would respond to your moves. There was none of the reserved Britishness you sometimes get in clubs in this green and pleasant land.

Well as you know, all good things must come to an end. Kate and my well worn-out shell went to the airport at midnight to say *adios* to James and *hola* to Tracy, who was staying with us for the second week. My last memory of the evening was trying to drink neat vodka which Tracy had got from duty-free. Uggghhh!

As I assumed the recovery position on Salinas beach the next day, I heard that Space had closed at two am and the party had continued at a local beach. I just chuckled to myself and let the sun bake my memories of what had been the party of the decade.

Colin Peters, London

'**Never get off the truck . . .**' The whisper was in my ear, but as I turned around, the voice melted into the crowd. What did it mean? It was only later, as we began to drift downstream through the sea of waving, whistling, screaming, wild humanity into our own heart of darkness and light, that I began to understand.

This was Love Parade '97, twice the size of the previous year, as always. Around one and a half million people were on the streets of Berlin for the biggest free party in Europe, the largest manifestation of house/techno culture the world has ever seen.

Our truck was the European House Connection featuring *DJ* Mag; Ministry of Sound; House-Frau and Freuden House; MTV; Unit Club, Hamburg; After Hour Power, Amsterdam; Great British Techno and Freie Manufactur.

The huge articulated lorry turned double-decker party sandwich, with scaffolding, a hot smelly generator and a huge sound system, was number thirty-five in a queue of forty such monsters. The parade was supposed to start at two pm, but because of the massive turn-out we didn't leave our spot in Otto-Suhr Alle to enter the madness of Ernst Peuter Platz, where the parade officially began, until four-thirty. The long wait, with the system turned off, created a strange, false sense of calm. DJ Frankie Foncett slept on the speakers and the transvestite dancers in the highest of heels and the smallest of PVC thongs ate bananas and drank Red Bull, steeling themselves for the show. We wandered along, lack of sleep making us light-headed, chatting to DJ Cirillo on the Coco Rico float, waving to the crew from Pioneer. A shrug and a smile. No need for words.

As we jumped back on the truck, just in time, we could see the hands flying into the air and feel the roar as truck number thirty-four eased into the crowd. Then, suddenly, after the endless waiting, we were on – awake, alive, loud and kicking.

Come on – PARTY, if we don't party, neither will they. That voice again, slipping away out of sight, as I stood on the top deck of the truck, dumbstruck, still, camera poised, staring at . . . people and more people. On the lamp-posts, on other trucks, on walls, on cars. There was no more space, nowhere else to go. *Never get off the truck . . . because if you get off you'll never get back on.* I completed the sentence for my spirit mentor. As we moved on down the Strasse Des 17 Juni the atmosphere slowly, imperceptibly changed. Charged, tribal, everybody on the truck was being drawn into the parade, becoming a part of the street theatre. Smiling, loosening up, grooving. *Let the sun shine in your heart,* the '97 motto, suddenly turned from a silly, hippie slogan into the perfect way of summing up the feeling. The sun shone, the systems pounded and we were all waving and screaming. And still we flowed on, the crowd swelling at the edges of the street, spilling over into the park and as far as anyone could see in every direction. There was no turning back, we had to roll forward into the depths of the groove.

Then it happened. A perfectly primal moment that loses so much in the retelling, but which has to be told. One of those what-is-he-on-about moments that so many clubbers experience the day after an ecstatic night.

Out of a near, clear blue sky, a patch of grey appeared and it started to rain on the parade, the sticky summer-heat sweat was washed away in a soaking, spirit-releasing shower. A photographer, after hurriedly packing his camera away, craned his neck skywards and opened his mouth wide to catch some raindrops. Everybody on the truck was screaming and waving and laughing. Yes – this is it . . . This is the moment of my life.

The rainbow described a perfect arc from the edge of the Tiergarten to the top of the Siegessaule, a golden angel saluting the shower. Then it was gone.

We had to duck to get under a railway bridge, shouting as loud as lungs can bear, underneath the metal. Then on towards the heart, the huge roundabout that surrounds the angel statue. And finally, suddenly, there we were, entering Grosser Stern. The sound switched from our own DJs to a radio signal, beamed to all of the trucks, linking the tribes to one fierce techno beat . . .
Christopher Mellor, DJ Magazine, London

This story is set in Manali in India, where the outdoor party scene is more active than Goa during the British summer. It's famous amongst the party crowd, although not so well known over here as its South Indian counterpart.

Over the hills where the spirits lie, the party people have come together to continue the story, the monsoon rains having driven them from the South. They are joined by others, freshly arrived from urban monotony, migrating in little groups to where the ringing mountains come and go in the clouds, the apples ripen on the trees, and the ice-melt river bursts its banks and munches up the roads. With no choice now, those who would never have found the motivation to leave anyway are trapped in this otherworld, where music never stops playing and the chillums are always alight . . .

It's a strange place in party season: beautiful as a dream, slow-paced and repetitive, the endless cycles of day and night rolling reality fluid in my mind. Two weeks there, and the cough begins, worsening inevitably with every chillum or bong until my lungs resign themselves to the adhesive coating of charas tar deposited every day. The days float by, drifting into each other in my memory. Time is marked by full moons, black moons, chance meetings with friends from another world, trips to the bank and the post office on a good day. And the parties: each slightly different from the countless that came before. Word spreads fast through the evolving community, and a talent develops for spotting the truth amongst the flourishing rumour.

foreign parts

We climb the mountainside, setting off too late and too stoned, with a bunch of people we've seen around and say they know the DJ. Not enough torches lurch in the darkness amongst the trees, unseen precipices suggested in the shadows; the sound of the river filling the cold air. We stumble along, one behind the other, a rainbow of languages and accents and laughter close by and murmuring out of sight. The path was lost way back: we heard that paint spots would mark the way but we think we've been following lichen for the last half an hour. Shouts come from above us, and we've got the right bloody mountain anyway.

The group halts, and some of us have disappeared. The remainder, drawn closer together, take a seat on the damp earth of the mountainside and spark up a chillum or two. Others emerge from below whilst we sit here, sweaty and unsuitably dressed, happy to find the consensus opinion is that the party's at the top of this one.

An hour further up, hoots ring out in the forest as we all hear the bass booming unmistakably through the trees. Enthusiasm rekindled, we strike straight upwards towards the sound, crawling on hands and knees through thistles, Himalayan nettles and minor land slips. The music draws us on more and more urgently as it gets louder and we can pick out the tunes. Great elation as some of us are fucked already. Pulling ourselves over the top, we find the place in full swing: a few locals making tea and eggs on a kerosene stove, tents and shelters and fires among the trees, the dancefloor and slightly flatter patch of mud between four large and battered speakers. One UV light blinks on and off, illuminating an alien drape ingeniously suspended. The site swarms with the dark shapes of people, and the 'Raelis are out in force under the stars. Dutch, English, Australian, French and Japanese do their thing. Trips and pills are bought and sold, given, shared and swapped, lost and found. Gear is everywhere. I'm up on my trip, the acid tension rising in my throat, making me laugh and bounce on the pine-covered ground when dodgy Ali who I know from last year says, *You know, I rrreally like this parrrty* in his to-die-for Iranian accent. Difficult to see who's who in this darkness; the whites of eyes flash and everyone's passing me chillums. I'm alright Jack whatever I am. Everyone's got their own view, but we're all hearing the same music, feeling the same rhythm; all of us are guests of this Full Moon, this mountain, following the patterns from moment to moment; we all know there's something we're celebrating.

And then the dawn comes. The stars have swept in their steady arc across the sky, and with them the moon, which is lost over the great shoulder of our hill. A greenish light grows across the valley, and shapes begin to appear out of the void. Gradually, colour creeps into my vision, first greys and blues and greens, and then the first tinges of yellow and pink. Movement and stillness, and a dawning difference; day opening like a lotus and the mountains are shining with gold. Everyone's trip turns as the sun strikes the tiny clearing in the woods, we all jump up to greet it, the music is playing and the party goes OFF! We're dancing in a paradise of trees and grass and ferns, the sky pulsing with blue and white, the sun glorious in our hair, the Indians dancing too now. The UV light is pale and unnecessary, forgotten now. We wander on the hillside, washing in the stream, meditating on the *beingness* of it all, always dancing too. Not so many of us now, since half went down again when the generator packed up during the night. But now the music is back, our boys have fixed it, and we are too happy for words.

Now we are bonded together, the ones left up here, and we shelter from the strengthening sun under a tree. We know we have to go down again sometime, because there's no water left so we're drinking from the stream. Don't really care, don't know the way down, and the clouds look like aliens and Shiva and dragons when I lie on my back. So much; there could be nothing at all, and there is so much, I think, and pass the chillum and flirt and watch the devil sticks twirled in the shade.

It's getting hot and somehow the music stops and we go, slipping and sliding and running down the hillside that's all green and reddish brown now. Passing patient cows and amused old cowherds and children who stare, we descend, each running with his private thoughts, stepping from here to there without thought, our natures and minds flowing perfectly, or so it seems to me. And then I'm alone, the others are gone somewhere, and it's right like that, because we're all alone, in the end. I laugh out loud, because I'm still tripping so I would think that. Acid days, acid dreams, Indian summers.

Anon

I went to Ibiza in 1991 for two weeks of non-stop partying. We didn't take any drugs with us; we didn't have to. You could get anything you wanted out there and it was cheaper and superior in quality to anything you could get here. We went to Space, which was indoors and there were thousands and thousands of people, all there to have a good time. It was amazing: the huge backdrops, lasers, strobes, inflatables … On the last day we realised we none of us had a sun tan because we'd been either sleeping or partying all day so we all made a concerted effort to get a tan and lay on the beach for a whole day and burnt ourselves to shit. Just to prove we'd been abroad.

Ralf E. P. (Oracle), Birmingham

Amnesia looks like a UFO has landed in the middle of a solitary Spanish hacienda. Kaleidoscopic lights glow from the centre of several thick white walls. Taxis and people in shorts and bright T-shirts mill around. It costs 4,000 pesetas to get in, which is about twenty quid and pretty steep.

The club, however, is kicking and almost full already. The decor is pure white and the dancefloor is open-air; stars twinkle crisply above.

The music is crisp and bright: . . . *n-n-numero, numero uno* . . . Chirpy pianos jump happily around. The club is full of colour with attractive people displaying lots of brown flesh and little self-consciousness. As Max and Ivan wade through the bopping

foreign parts

crowd they see bandannas, swimming goggles, Kickers, cowboy hats, bikinis and Indian gear.

The dancefloor is packed but relatively cool, because there's no ceiling to keep the hot sweat in. As if on cue, a new and dynamite tune comes on as they reach the dancefloor: . . . *afro, afro-dizzy-at* . . . Epic drums pump and power on: . . . *why do dat doo di* . . . Max and Ivan are instantly rushing. Suddenly, they're really there, in the thick of it: . . . *volla de shazback* . . . Max grins up at the open night's sky and jacks his body. Ivan treads on several people's toes in his exuberance.

A sample of Humphrey Bogart in *The African Queen* rumbles out of the speakers: *Shall we drop the anchor sweetheart? . . . You promised you'd go down the river*, Katharine Hepburn stridently replies. *Then down the river we go . . .*

A few small white flecks float down from the night sky and rest on Max's smiling, upturned face. At first he thinks it's his imagination, or something trippy going on. Then he wonders whether it's snow. Snow? In Ibiza in midsummer? Gradually, the white fluffy blobs float down in increasing intensity. Max is totally puzzled. He wipes his finger along the bare midriff of a girl in a shiny bikini dancing near him. She doesn't notice. He gazes at the evidence dangling off his finger. *What's this?* he asks Ivan. *Dunno. It's everywhere tho', innit.*

Looking around, they spot a cannon perched next to the DJ booth overlooking the dancefloor. It's pumping increasingly large quantities of foam over the clubbers. The voices of Bogart and Hepburn reappear amongst the strummed guitar riffs. *How do you like it?* Bogart asks excitedly. *Like it?* she replies incredulously. *I never dreamed any mere physical experience could be so stimulating . . .*

The white bubbles have started to accumulate on the floor and over everyone. Like the shower at the end of the night at E's Paradis, it has a liberating effect, unleashing any remaining inhibitions. Ivan slips and is momentarily lost under the encroaching sea of foam. Various limbs and bits of bodies emerge and disappear into the fluffy tide. Max kills himself laughing as a virtually unrecognisable Ivan rubs froth out of his eyes. The geezer in swimming goggles suddenly looks like he's got the right idea.

'French Kiss' comes on. This minimal and notoriously sexy track is number one in the charts back home in Britain. Everyone goes loopy, bouncing up and down. On and around the raised platform in the centre of the dancefloor vain and beautiful people gyrate. Girls with long blonde hair in skimpy revealing tops rub shoulders with muscular and topless young men. Bodies jerk to the sparse and heavy beat. Everyone is smiling, looking around, together in enjoyment of the experience.

Another piano-led record breaks in. A fierce black female voice booms, *'Cos you're RIGHT on time!* . . . Everyone's totally up for it as dawn surreptitiously creeps up.
Daniel Newman, London

Bali, Indonesia. Inspirational island images of bright white sand and a subculture of fish slithering in shoals through the sea, evoke impressions of idyllic tranquillity and fertility. For those brought up on British club culture, the Hindu-influenced Back to Basics lifestyle thwarts all thoughts of Bali and relocates the mind in Leeds, UK. Oppositions exist; these are two cultures without room for coalition.

However, contemporary Bali is not tied to tradition. Its Back to Basics ethos has accommodated European expectations, entrepreneurial natives quickening the nation's evolution by aiding travellers in the late sixties to experience Bali's spiritual ecstasy. Since then, the essence of ecstasy has evolved and Balinese entrepreneurs are fast erecting four walls within which a chemically-concocted utopia can be captured.

As a backpacker, far-flung from beats per minute, stumbling upon a club scene creates a somewhat authentic sensation, like sixties' surfers discovering sets of rideable waves in Kuta. For the Back to Basics girl in Bali, however, the vibe is not a remix of an inner-city superclub. The lunacy of enduring inevitably bad English weather to enter a club contrasts with the ease of waiting to dance in Bali. A novel sensation attacks bare skin: warmth. Past the doors, space and the set played are certainly smaller, yet not sobering. The spirit of beachside Club 66 is spared the tension of people released from the restrictive rules of work. Upheld by Hinduism not capitalism, the national Balinese values of optimism and harmony imbue its clubs. A shared sense of good times is spiritually available, or sold in amphetamine form: the hedonism is infectious. Accustomed to feeling disorientated and down by the reality that outside home clubs this spirit is

dead, the uplifting Balinese mood transgresses the walls and remains while you bike it back along the beach to the bungalow.
Natalie, Marlow

I'm here to reprazent the black and the Asian crew. It ain't just a WASP thing, not all niggaz is gangstas! Respect Frankie Knuckles, respect Carl Cox, respect Asian Dub Foundation and all the other posses out there. You know the score.

We been in NYC, we been in Detroit, we been in Cally, and they ain't doing it like we doing it in the UK. Here our friends are Ebenezer and Billy, but those kids are tight with my man Charlie every night, you know what I'm saying! And there ain't no underground like we got. There's the rich kids, the valley kids and the college kids doing it; that's one thing that ain't bigger and better over there.

Here we got the jungle, we got the drum and bass, we got the ragga, we got the triphop, we got the bhangra stylee. We ain't just the MCs to the white kid, always giving it that 'booyaka' thing no more. In the US of A they got soul. We got that too.

We all part of this scene too, you better hear me. Respect the black crew; the UK's the place to be, know what I'm saying?

Peace, brothers and sisters.

Out.
Anon

'Out There' Techno Festival: Gorron, France, July 1997: Arrive on Thursday evening in Caen and hitch a lift with a lorry-load of Londoners. As we approach the site it begins to rain. Emma sets up a shelter by the river. I set off with ten cans of her lager to sell but become her best customer. Consequently, the first night is a blur of events and people: jamming jungle bass on a synth; attempting a turn at DJing and hearing, *Don't let her on, she's a fucking nutter!*; rolling naked as the dawn rose in the dewy grass with a passing stranger.

Friday: we retire from the rain inside Emma's construction of tarpaulin, plastic, wood, cardboard and string. My contribution is a loo-roll holder, also made of string . . .

Friday night: still raining. Admire my new raincoat made from bin-bag. Emma is eager for us to be fluorescently painted so we can find each other in the dark. But as we keep falling out, this idea soon becomes redundant. I become very attracted to the face-painter's fire, so I linger, drink brandy coffee, give a massage and chill . . . for a while at least.

Midnight: a Bristolian gets me climbing to the top of a small marquee tent and there we sit watching proceedings like king and queen with a spliff.

Find a tent and trance out to the layers of fast winding, twirling, industrialesque, macho, militant, thudding, feel-it-in-your-groin sound. Close eyes . . . Whiteness . . . I am on a conveyor belt and it's up to me to create the scenery that flashes by.

Beyond daybreak, Saturday: disentangle myself from my trance state, but only because the tent is being taken down. I stumble outside into sunlight and encounter a most gorgeous Frenchman. We chat whilst I try and suppress sudden feelings of shyness. He leaves saying we will have a good dance together tonight.

Midnight, Saturday: microdot time – taking great care not to lose mine as Emma did hers! Go wandering and find myself in the Hypnotic Unity tent. Whilst amongst the unity of the hypnotised, gorgeous Frenchman appears. We smile at each other ... eye contact of a serious dimension occurs ... I am flying.

Crash landing: a chain of events finds me alone and sad in a café tent, but not for long. Two French friends talk about their brotherly love and share their whisky with me. One gives me *such* a blowback that I name him Dragon-Man. Two Eastenders join us with triple-strength brandy coffee. They also have a brotherly love friendship. I feel warm inside and surrounded by warmth. Meanwhile, one of the Eastenders tries to lean against a bar that isn't there!

I wander back to the deserted Hypnotic Unity tent (!) hoping to be magically reunited with the gorgeous Frenchman. Instead, a man hunting for sex latches on to me ... A psychic friend told me once that she could see a hole near my shoulder, possibly caused by a spear in a former life ... This guy points to the exact spot and asks, *What is this?*

Sunday morning: find a hill and open a bottle of Chianti. I have also found myself a 'warrior stick'. A woman (who likes to carry a toy dog) stops to admire the way you can squat and lean against its curve. Then a French guy stops for a lean on it and talks about the importance of uplifting contact between people.

Sunday evening: hear of a party at the weekend, plan to AWOL from work with food-poisoning and earn money litter-picking . . . Become paranoid that I might actually get it as punishment for having pretended food-poisoning. Then I meet a guy who just so happens to have a herbal cure for food-poisoning with him. He talks about how technology has suppressed the earth's natural magic.

Monday: link up with Toy Dog Woman and friend. Both have found themselves a warrior stick (I've lost mine). We set off on a mission to watch the sunset from the top of a wooded hill. Also with us are some children, a woman with masses of material in her hair and Brian from the London lorry contingent.

Lots of diversions and confusions occur on our mission. Some drama crossing the river, and when we finally get to the top we can't see much through the trees anyway.

Back at the river it's just me and Brian (the others disappeared one by one into the shaded sunset). Somehow we've both ended up with the other people's warrior sticks, whilst the Material Hair Woman has my jumper and Toy Dog Woman has Brian's T-shirt.

Brian shares his remaining drugs with me and we head for the main arena. It has become full of rubbish, and fires are raging with lots of plastic shit thrown on them. The air reeks with paraffin as fire jugglers come out in force.

Dilettante Di, Hove

Club Vaudeville, Brussels: To enter this former theatre you have to pass the Galeries de la Reine – an Art Deco corridor with a glass roof and shops on both sides. In between two shops there's a small entrance to the Vaudeville. My girlfriend's clothing is kinda special tonight – she looks like a transvestite. Lucky, since this is a gay club. Between the entrance and the main dancefloor there's a room filled with seats and practically no lights. We cross these ten metres and get left and right glimpses of bodies entangled in each other. White powder-lines are displayed on the tables.

At the bar we order a drink and look around. We see people dressed up in baby dolls and moon boots, others in a French cancan suit. Most of them wear designer clothes or sexshop outfits, giant hats and tons of make-up. Some look like business men – but don't act like them. The men's bathroom is crowded. The opposite sex's is almost empty. The music is quite hard: acid and Belgian R&S-techno *avant la lettre*.

We go to the dancefloor and meet some friends. I buy some poppers at the men's room. Inhaling it through nose or mouth makes your skin glow. An energy flash combusts in your belly and rushes to your head. It's like your body temperature rises twenty degrees in fifteen seconds. Music seems to echo inside your head.

Light-effects become fireworks. The effect lasts for sixty seconds, no longer, but enough to get you in the groove. Inhaling it makes you want to laugh, really laughing your heart out. Me and my girlfriend pass the poppers on to each other, others dancing take a sniff out of our bottle and soon ten or more people on the dancefloor are laughing, dancing, making funny faces.

Suddenly, the pounding beat stops and the sound of the French cancan hits the room. On stage ten go-go 'girls' start dancing as if they were in the Moulin Rouge itself. Amongst them there's the guy with the baby doll and moon boots. Dancing the cancan with moon boots seems not that easy and after a few seconds the first moon boot is ejected into space over our heads and lands safely in the bar. The other one, although successfully launched, was never recovered.

Meanwhile, the effect of the poppers was still lasting and we were lying down on the dancefloor having cramps from laughing. The bottle being passed on from one hand made our minds go wild. My cheeks hurt from laughing. The next song the DJ played was 'You're The One That I Want' from the movie *Grease*. Everybody went wild and the whole club was aroused.

This was the age of pure decadence: bodies almost naked, people of all genders making love, drugs freely available, techno pounding, lights flashing. Free your mind and the rest will follow.

Needless to say, the police shut down the club after a *razzia* some months later.

Gery & Wendy, Belgium

For a DJ, New Year's Eve is more like a sleep deprivation experiment than a party. This was the plan: fly from London to Rome; drive to Naples before midnight when the people have a tendency to throw large bombs and fridges on to passing cars; DJ at Dynamik Area some time after two am when it is once again sort of safe to go out; catch Tony Humphries' set at another club between seven am and eleven am; drive back to Rome; get back on a plane and fly home, back in time for *ET* on the telly. You'll notice in there the lack of key words like hotel, rest, sleep; add a serious case of cold/flu to this punishing schedule and you end up with twenty-four hours mostly spent trying to grab a few minutes' sleep on various uncomfortable chairs for lengths of time just too short to actually drop off, or standing around in nightclubs trying to work out exactly what was happening and, more importantly, who had the free drink tickets.

So was it worth it? Of course it bloody was, for those little moments that stick in the memory more than not being able to breathe properly, trying not to cough in a car full of smokers and wandering round the duty-free looking like an unshaven ghost. Like these: being assigned my own personal bodyguard for the journey across the dancefloor at Dynamik Area (and only later wondering why I would need one); wondering who the two dorky-looking blokes DJing were, then finding out they were Deep Dish; hearing the MC (and half the crowd) sing along to all-time house classic 'Promised Land': Tony Humphries spinning 'The World is a Ghetto' and getting the whole crew back on their feet at ten am; bouncing over the bumps in the back streets in the back of a stretch-limo with big Tony and an even bigger bottle of champagne; finally crashing out on the plane on the way home and dreaming about ... well, that's another story.

Christopher Mellor, DJ Magazine, London

Fuckin' hell, we're in New York! was the catchphrase of the holiday. The highpoint: Junior Vasquez at The Tunnel, which was mainly why we went. It was too late to catch him at The Sound Factory, which had closed down some months before, so it wasn't quite like that 'Englishman in New York' tune, but it was certainly the next best thing.

I'd been following Junior's career for some time. Okay, it sounds a bit passé now, but let's remember that at the time he was THE MAN – and you had absolutely no chance of hearing him play unless you went to New York, because he just didn't tour. Junior certainly knew a thing or two about creating a legend about himself.

My interest came from having basically been a complete NY house junkie for several years. My mate Darren's came from when he used to put parties on in the huge flat he lived in, which I used to DJ at. *The* big tune was always 'Get Your Hands off my Man' (most of the rest of my set used to comprise of Vasquez mixes as well, come to that). So when it came to picking a holiday destination, yeah, we thought about Ibiza, but why go to Ibiza with everyone else to hear DJs you could hear at home, when you could spend the same money getting to the Big Apple and see a DJ you knew no one else had? Seemed straightforward enough to us.

So we've been in NYC nearly a week. It's been a top holiday all round: lots of sightseeing by day and lots of drinking by night. We've been to the Eightball shop and gotten all excited (and I've still got the carrier bag to this day); we've done all the touristy stuff, and we've bought lots of designer clothes at ridiculously low prices. We've wandered around Greenwich Village and fallen in love every fifteen yards (where do all those beautiful women come from?); we've managed to score some top-flight weed off a nice student girl with beautiful almond-shaped brown eyes. Couldn't have been much better, really.

And now it's Saturday night, and this is what we've been waiting for. We're in our room at the Vanderbilt Y getting ready. Now, we're both veteran clubbers of some years' standing, but this is something special, and we're both getting really stupidly excited – I reckon we've both gotten changed about eight times. We have a slight dilemma 'cos we ended up with Darren in cream jeans and a black T-shirt and me in black jeans and a cream T-shirt, but eventually decide it's kind-of-cool so we stick with that and go hail a cab.

The yellow cab drives through one of the seedier fringes of Manhattan before pulling up outside a pair of big warehouse-style doors, outside which are bouncers, velvet ropes and one of the longest queues you've ever seen. One bouncer detaches himself from the group, comes over to our cab and opens the doors for us (you know, like they do all the time in England – yeah *right*), saying *Welcome to The Tunnel* – cool! (and then, lower, *Tip me guys,* when we nearly don't, oh well), and there we are. We're at The Tunnel.

That's *at,* not *in.* There's still the little matter of that queue, to the back of which we obediently trudge – and Christ, that's practically a walking holiday in itself. What's all the more upsetting is that the queue's full of such uninteresting people: really bad European-tourist types in blue jeans, red-and-yellow anoraks, Rucanor rucksacks even. Don't these people have a clue? Anyone who looks even remotely like you'd expect New York clubbers to look is either walking straight in at the front or getting pulled out by the picker and ushered in. Memories of queuing outside Vague and getting a knockback come flooding back and I'm thinking, no, we're just not gonna let that happen. We've come three thousand miles for this, for fuck's sake.

So the picker walks by again, for probably the third or fourth time: this absolutely enormous black guy, shaven head, collar-to-ankle fur coat, and camp as Christmas. *Excuse me,* I say, and he stops and strolls over, *Are we in the right line here?*

And he looks me up and down and says, *Well who are you with, honey?*

And I say, *Just this gentleman here,* and he looks Darren up and down, and his face goes from bitchy queen to big welcoming smile and he says, *Follow me, guys . . .*

And he lifts the velvet rope and we duck under and follow him up the inside lane, past all the rednecks and gawpers, and he walks us through the doors and tells the cashier, *It's fifteen dollars for these two, okay?* (it's meant to be twenty), and we pay our money, and just before we walk in through the interior doors, I look at Darren and he looks at me, and we're both, like, *Fuckin' hell! We're in!* and then Darren's saying, *I bet everyone we know would like to be us right at this moment,* and then as we open those interior doors we're just like, *Jesus . . .*

I've been to some clubs, but Christ! The place is huge, and incredibly aptly named – it really is a long, thin tunnel. All the bar women look like Lady Miss Kier and the lights are fantastic. We're impressed. Then we find the side rooms: no scruffy old torn sofas in here, but ultra-modern glass tables and white leather settees and fluorescent uplights and . . . it's just club heaven, it's perfect. And the sound! There's just the one sound system throughout (no 'back room' in the traditional sense) but everywhere you go it's absolutely crystal, there's speakers everywhere.

Then we go upstairs. It's a bit perturbing to wander up the stairs and find yourself in the bogs. It's even more perturbing that the bogs are completely open plan: you have to walk through the men's to get to the ladies', not that anyone's really paying any attention to which is which. The only difference is that in the ladies' you can have a bit of a make-over, while in the men's bit there's a barber's chair if you fancy a shave. But the weirdest thing of all is the bar that's slap-bang in between the two: a bar in the toilets, complete with white-tiled walls and floors. We're looking at each other and we're just shaking our heads in disbelief with these huge grins on our faces. What a club! We wander round some more and we find a lounge-bar type area where we have a sit down, and a waitress comes over and takes our drinks orders. A waitress!

We spend a good hour or so running round the club trying to get hold of a few certain little extras – a very kooky Japanese girl with a velvet top-hat and a cane who we meet in the lounge-bar eventually obliges, although the weird thing is how socially unacceptable the question seems to be. I mean, we're being polite about it and everything! But there you go, that's New Yorkers for you: friendly as anything when they want to be, cool as ice when they don't. Whatever, we manage in the end. And all the time Junior's working, working those tunes: he's keeping a groove going with one tune, a bassline and a vocal sample for like twenty minutes, half an hour. All of it as funky as fuck. Awesome.

We sit in the lounge bar and try and get our heads round it all. We're in New York. We're in The Tunnel. We've just necked a pill. And Junior's not just living up to expectations, he's exceeding them by several degrees of magnitude. We look at each other. We nod.

And we go off to the dancefloor and dance our tits off all night. Well I mean, what would you do?
Russell David, Bath